Fifty (50) states make up the United States (U.S). There are 16 U.S. territories. Five are always inhabited. This activity book will help you explore the map of the United States.

Instructions

1. On the map of the United States **look** for the bullseye. *Note: Instead of looking all over the map the bullseye narrows your search. See Figure 1. Example of Bullseye.*

2. Color the picture of the state shown above the map. The color of the state should be the same color as the state on the map (see the example on the next page).

3. Next, in the area identified as the bullseye, **find** the state mentioned on the page. For example, if the state you are looking at is Alabama, on the map of the United States, in the bullseye, you should see the state of Alabama; **shade** it in with your crayon or color pencil (see the example on the next page). Note: If you need help finding the state in the bullseye, refer to the labeled map on the last page.

4. You can **color** the state's favorite food(s) or any other picture on the page.

Figure 1. Bullseye Example

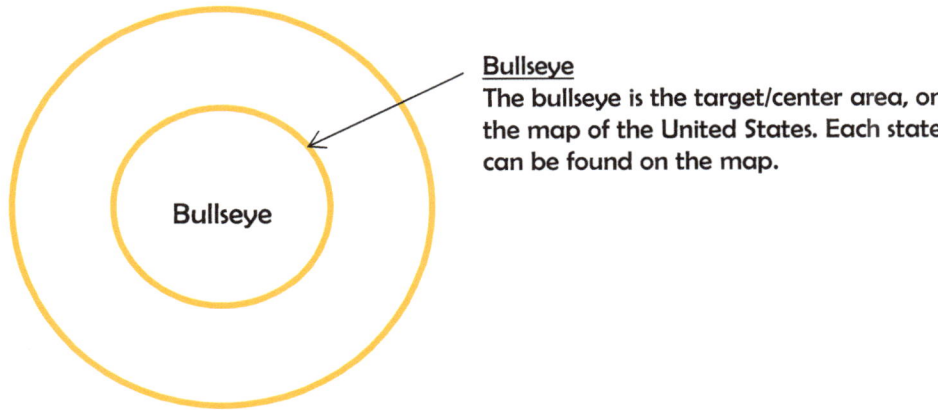

Bullseye
The bullseye is the target/center area, on the map of the United States. Each state can be found on the map.

© 2018 DigiAuthors production. All Rights Reserved. SPOT and all related titles, logos, are trademarks of DigiAuthors and IMD company.

1. Alabama

Nickname: Yellowhammer State

Example

1. Color the state ⟶

2. Find it on the map.

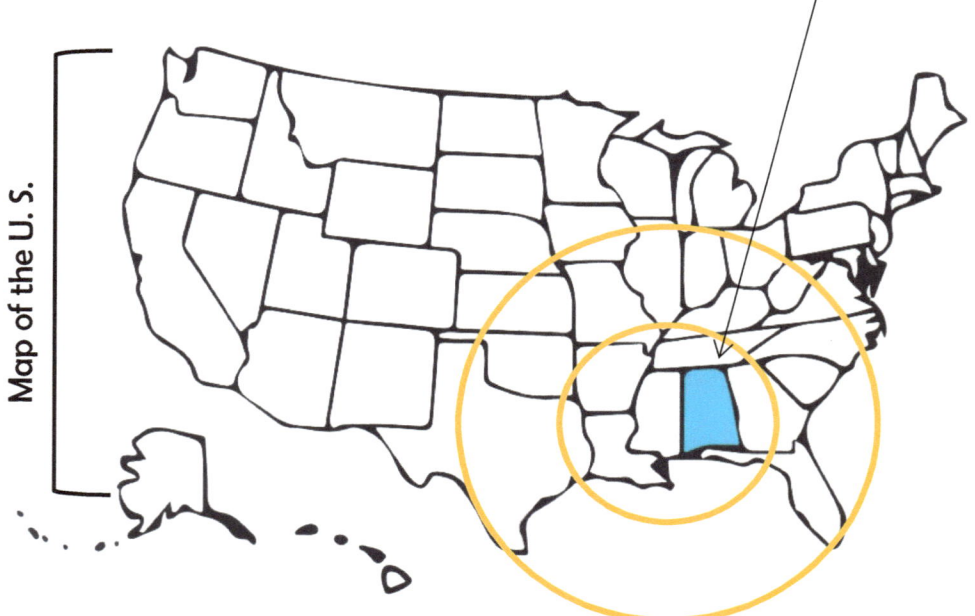

Map of the U. S.

CAPITAL: Montgomery

Start your day with creamy cheese and grits.

2. Alaska

Nickname: The Last Frontier

CAPITAL: Juneau

Alaskan Salmon, a favorite meal at dinner time, served with mashed potatoes, rice, or pasta.

3. Arizona

Nickname: The Grand Canyon State

CAPITAL: Phoenix

Arizonians love Mexican food. You can fill your plate with nachos, burritos, and enchiladas.

4. Arkansas

Nickname: The Natural State

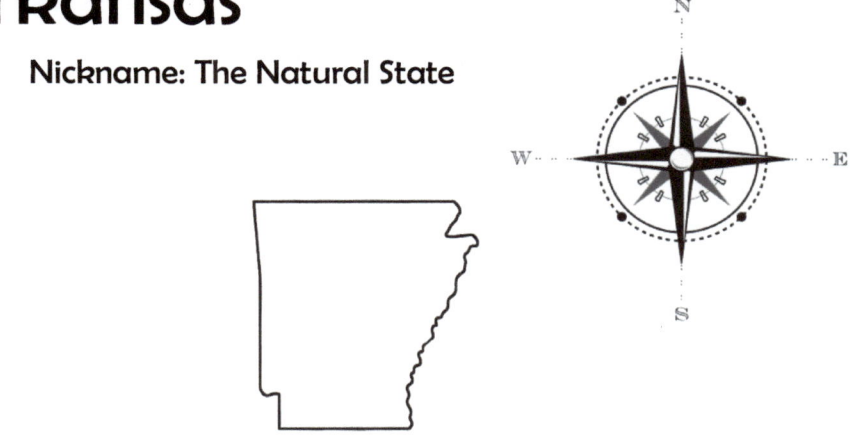

CAPITAL: Little Rock

Cheese dips are famous during the Super Bowl.

5. California

Nickname: The Golden State

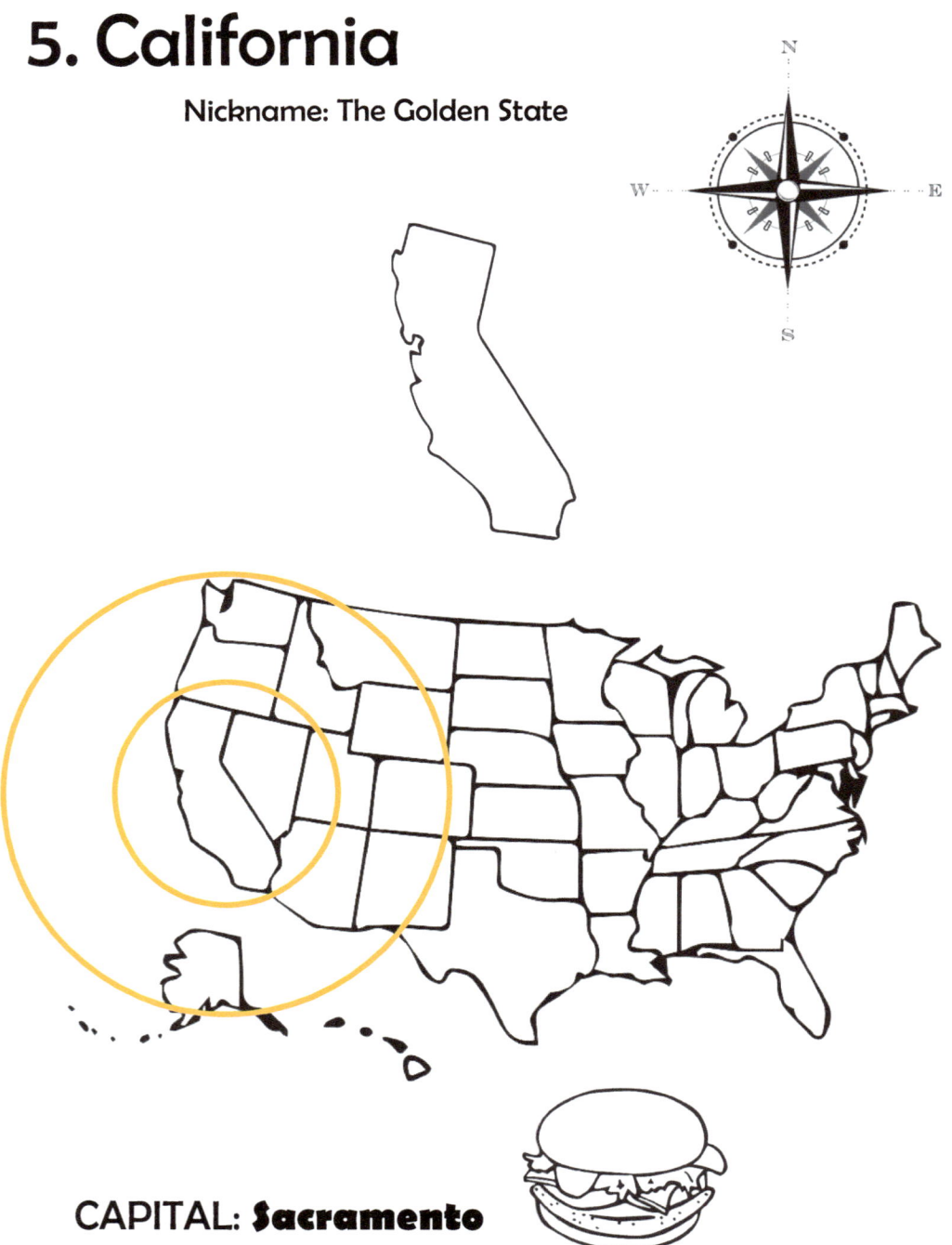

CAPITAL: Sacramento

Californians love burgers served with French fries.

6. Colorado

Nickname: The Centennial State

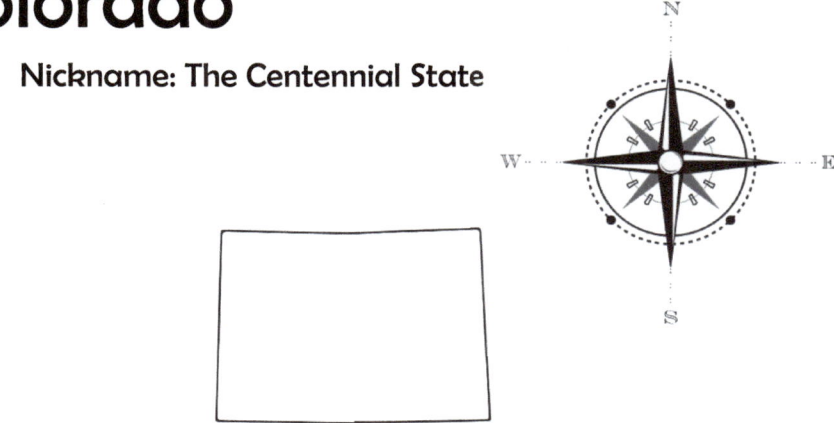

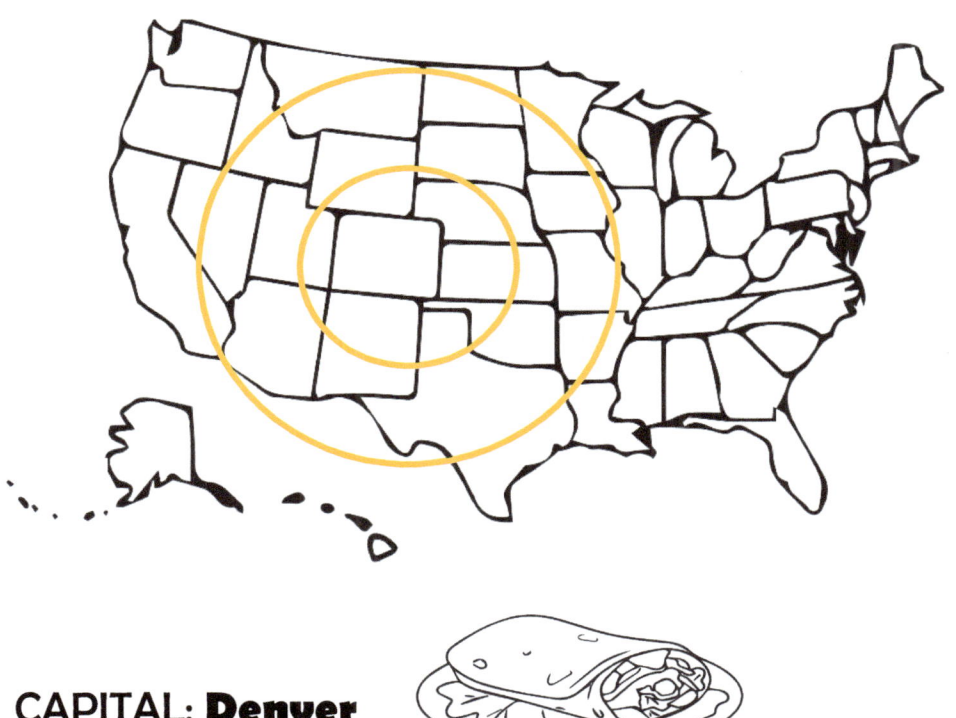

CAPITAL: Denver

Beef enchiladas are a favorite in this state. Serve it with rice, beans, and tomato sauce.

7. Connecticut

Nickname: The Constitution State

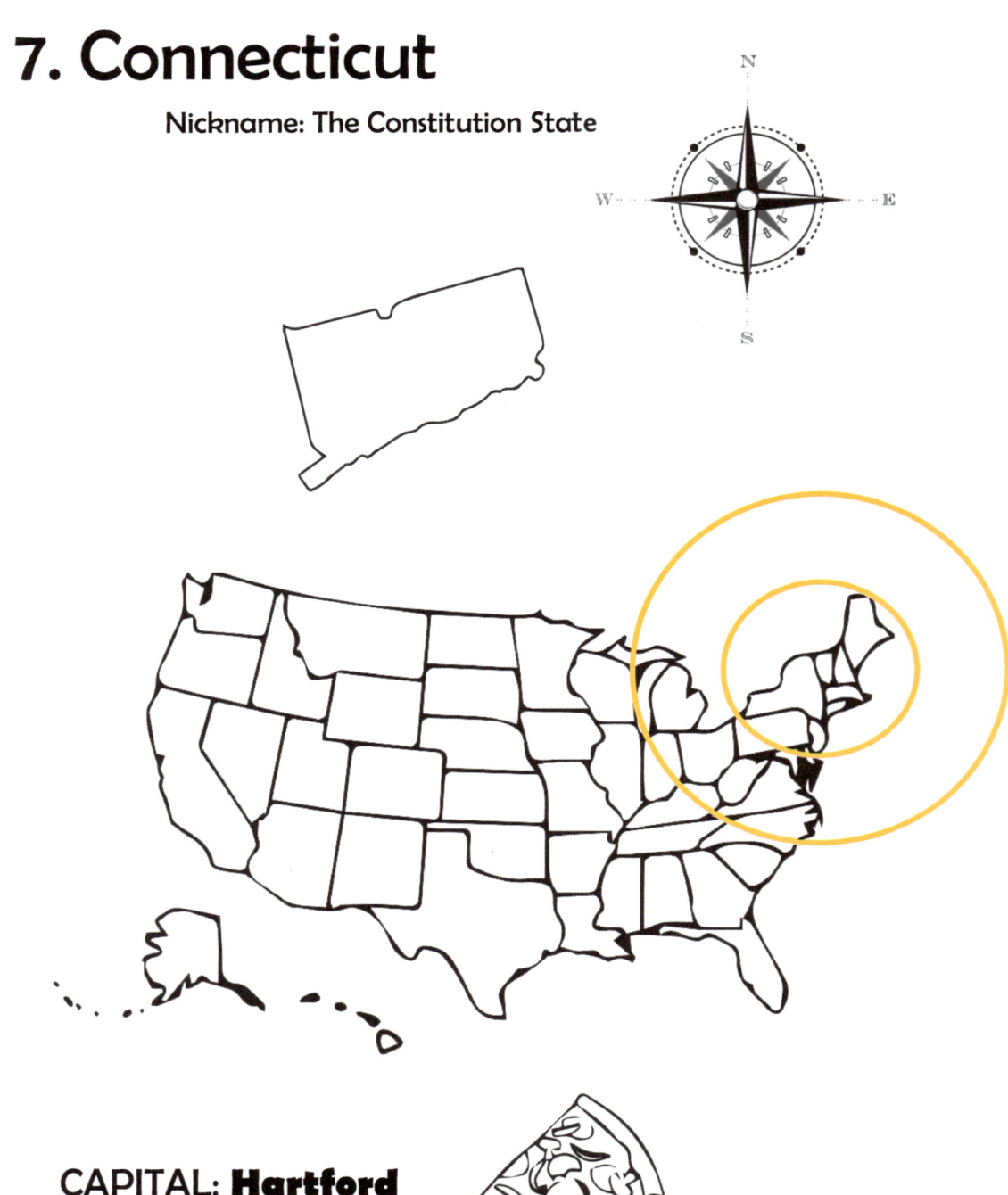

CAPITAL: Hartford

In Connecticut, pizza brings family and friends together.

8. Delaware

Nickname: The First State

CAPITAL: Dover

In this state, chicken is cooked in so many ways: roasted, fried, and baked.

9. Florida

Nickname: The Sunshine State

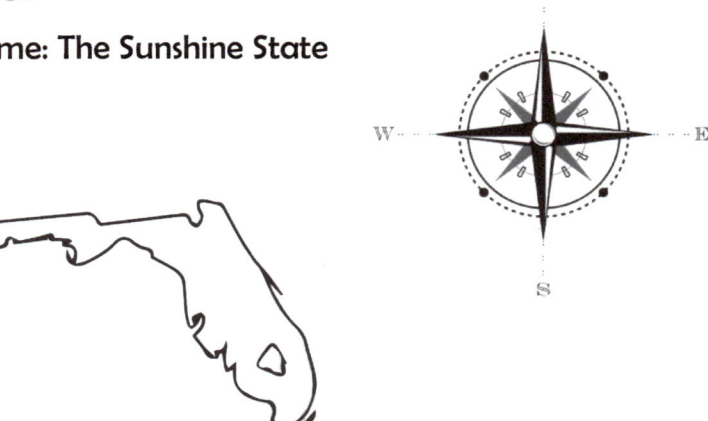

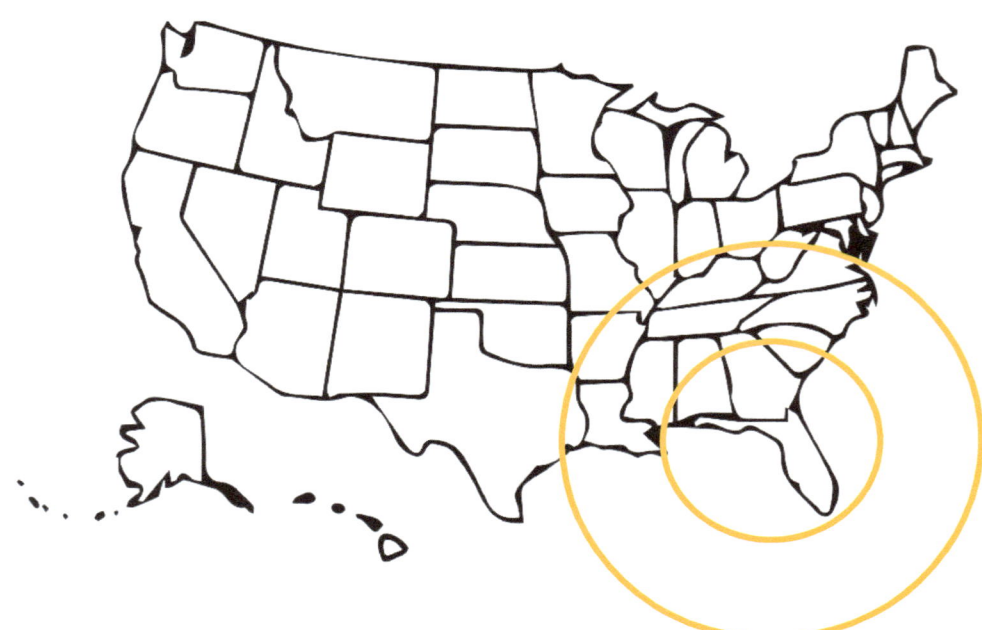

CAPITAL: Tallahassee

In Florida, you can experience Cuban cuisines such as: beans and rice, pork, and chicken.

10. Georgia

Nickname: The Peach State

CAPITAL: Atlanta

For dessert order, Georgia's peach cobbler, topped with vanilla ice cream.

11. Hawaii

Nickname: The Aloha State

CAPITAL: Honolulu

Hawaiians love SPAM. SPAM sandwich, SPAM and rice, or SPAM and peas.

12. Idaho

Nickname: The Gem State

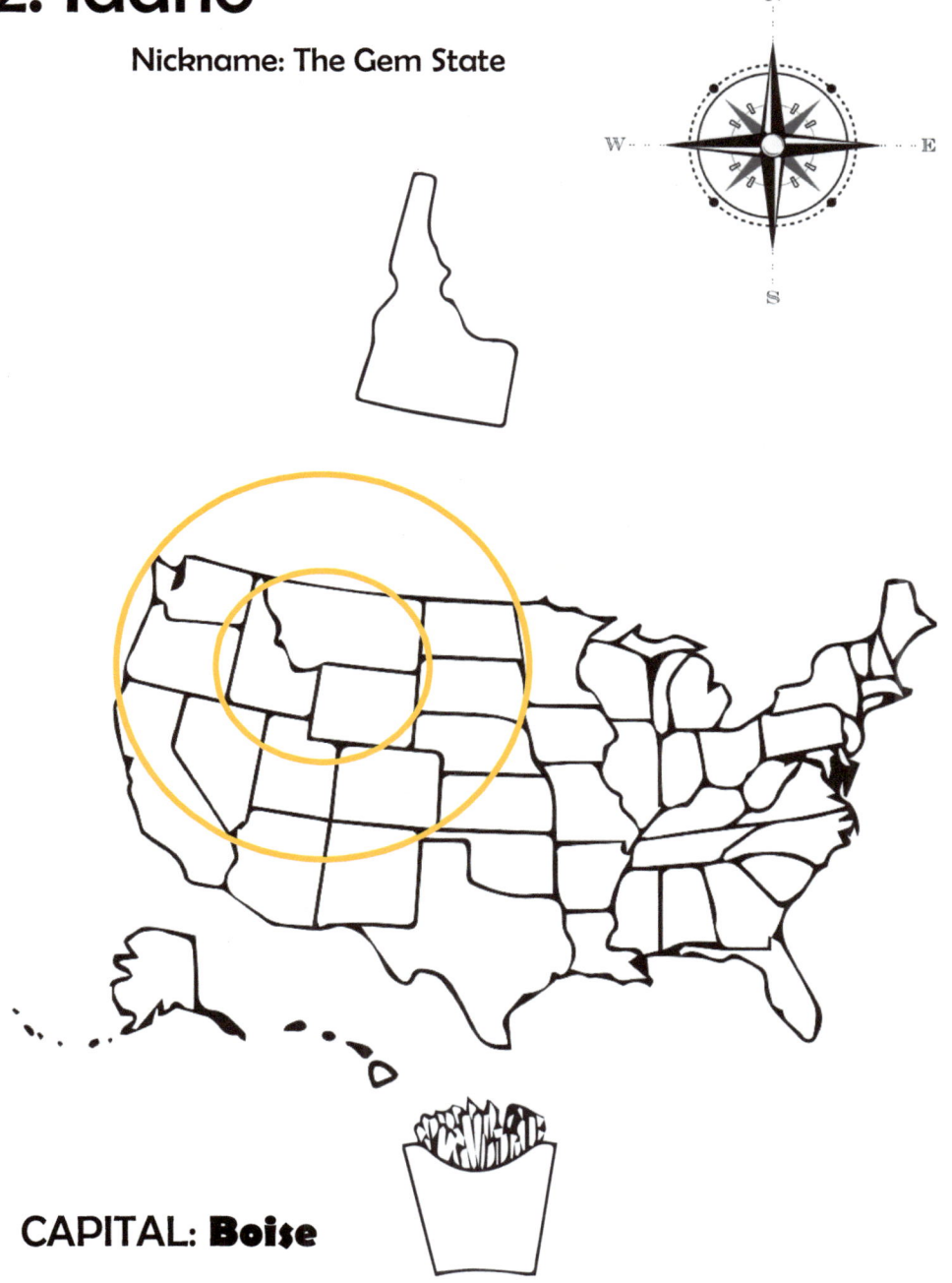

CAPITAL: Boise

Idaho is known for its potatoes. They make good French fries and tater tots.

13. Illinois

Nickname: Prairie State

CAPITAL: Springfield

In this state you can fill your belly with delicious meat dishes.

14. Indiana

Nickname: The Hoosier State

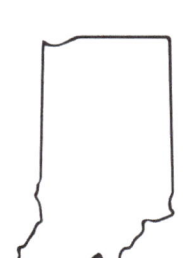
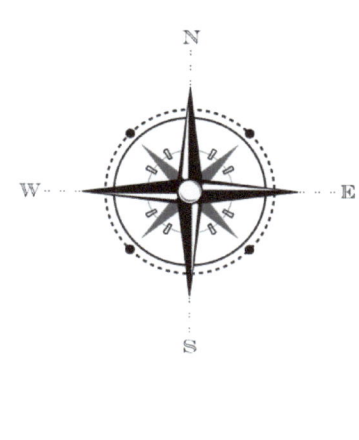

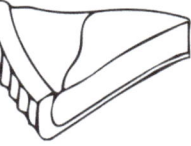

CAPITAL: **Indianapolis**

Indiana has the best sugar cream pie. During Thanksgiving, you can smell fresh backed sugar cream pie in grandma's kitchen.

15. Iowa

Nickname: The Hawkeye State

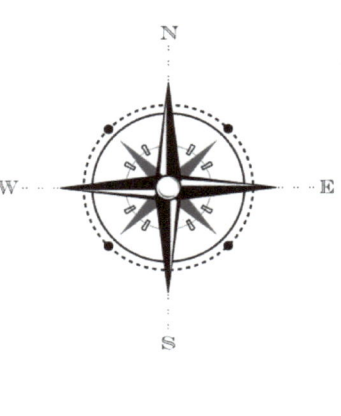

CAPITAL: Des Moines

Corn is the best crop to grow in Iowa. In the summer cook it on the grill, add it to your favorite dish.

16. Kansas

Nickname: The Sunflower State

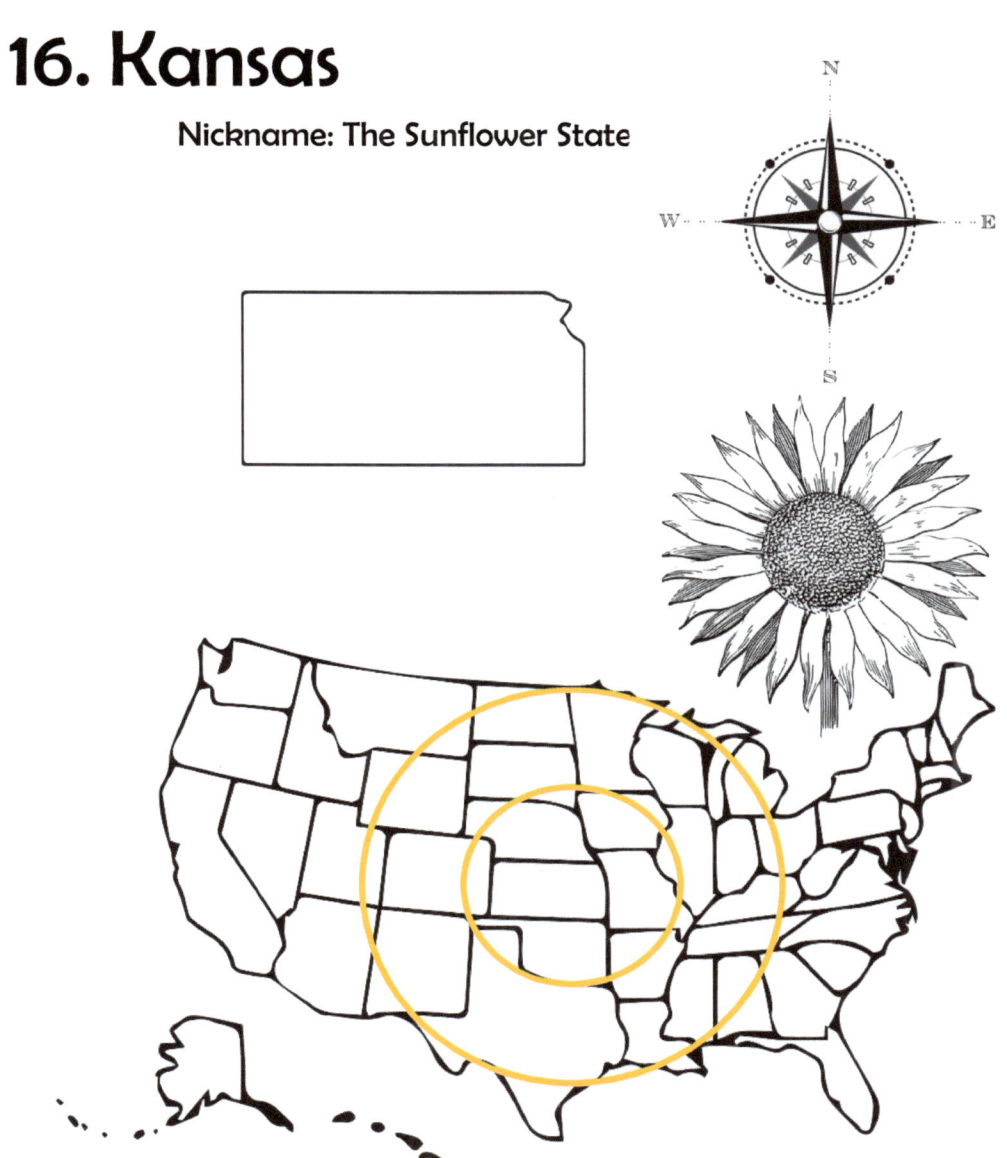

CAPITAL: Topeka

Kansas is also known as the "breadbasket" state.

17. Kentucky

Nickname: The Bluegrass State

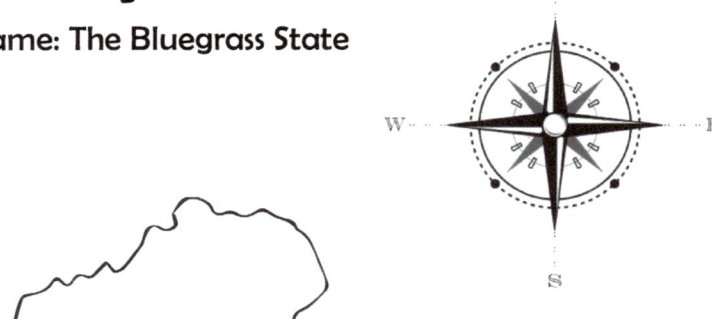

CAPITAL: Frankfort

Everyone loves Kentucky's fried chicken.

18. Louisiana

Nickname: The Pelican State

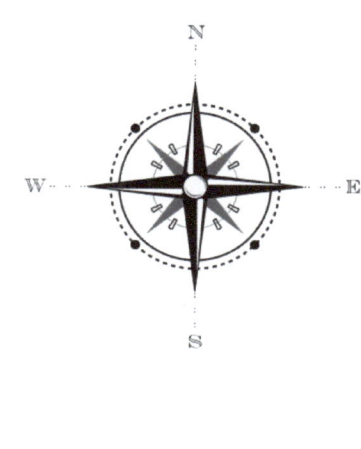

CAPITAL: **Baton Rouge**

Seafood, such as shrimp, lobster, oysters, fish, and crab, are favorite foods in this state.

19. Maine

Nickname: The Pine Tree State

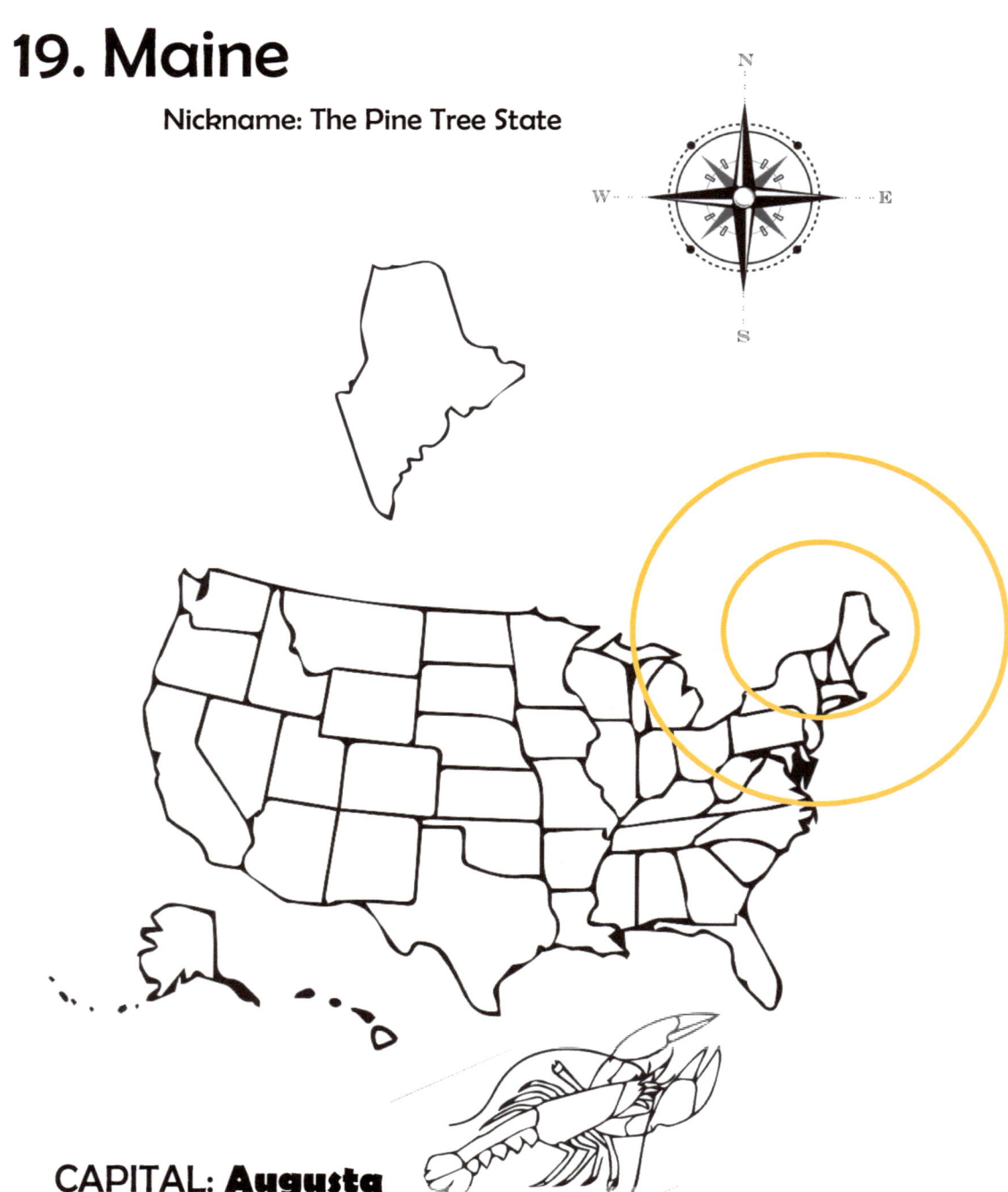

CAPITAL: Augusta

Maine has the best lobster dishes. Try a lobster roll the next time you're in town.

20. Maryland

Nickname: The Old Line State

CAPITAL: Annapolis

In this state, flavored crabs are common.

21. Massachusetts

Nickname: The Bay State

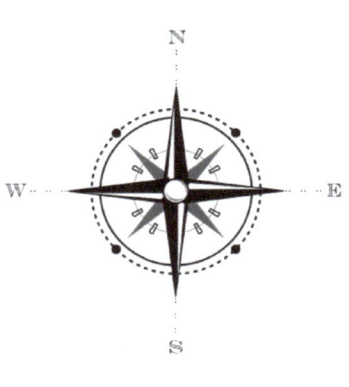

CAPITAL: Boston

In Massachusetts, the soup of the day is Clam Chowder.

22. Michigan

Nickname: The Great Lakes State

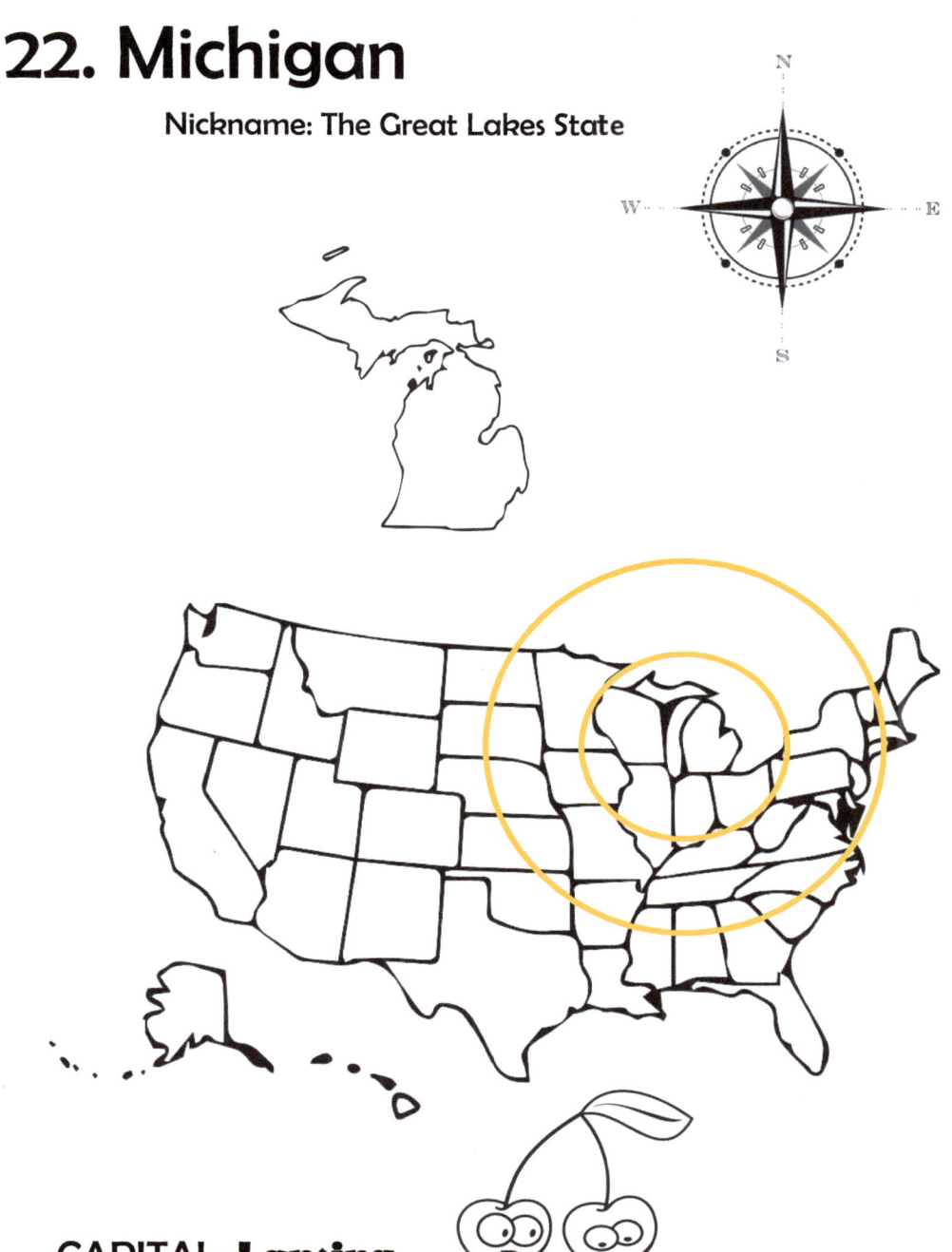

CAPITAL: Lansing

In Michigan, cherries make a delicious cherry pie.

23. Minnesota

Nickname: The North Star State

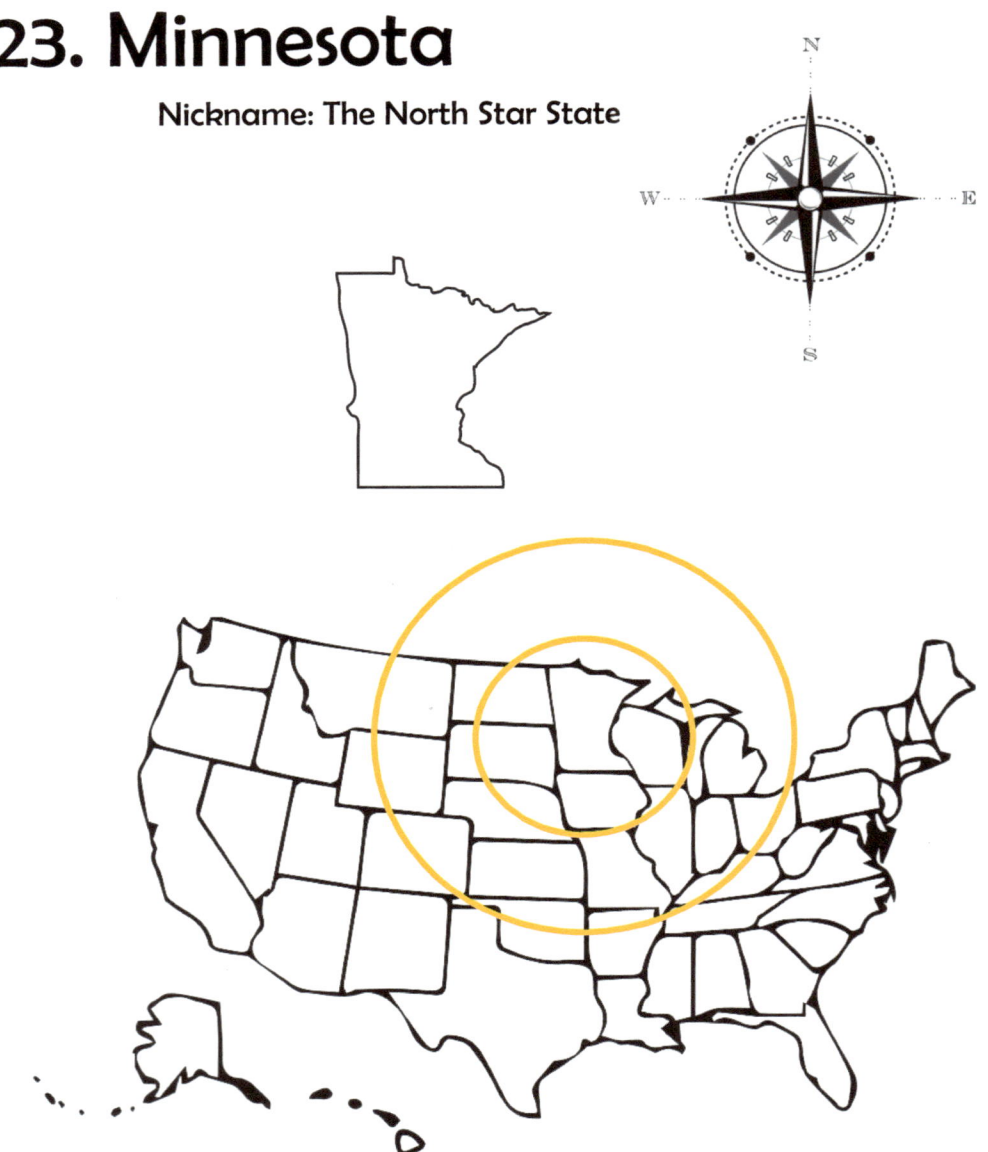

CAPITAL: St. Paul

Hot tater tots; serve them for breakfast, lunch, or dinner.

24. Mississippi

Nickname: The Magnolia State

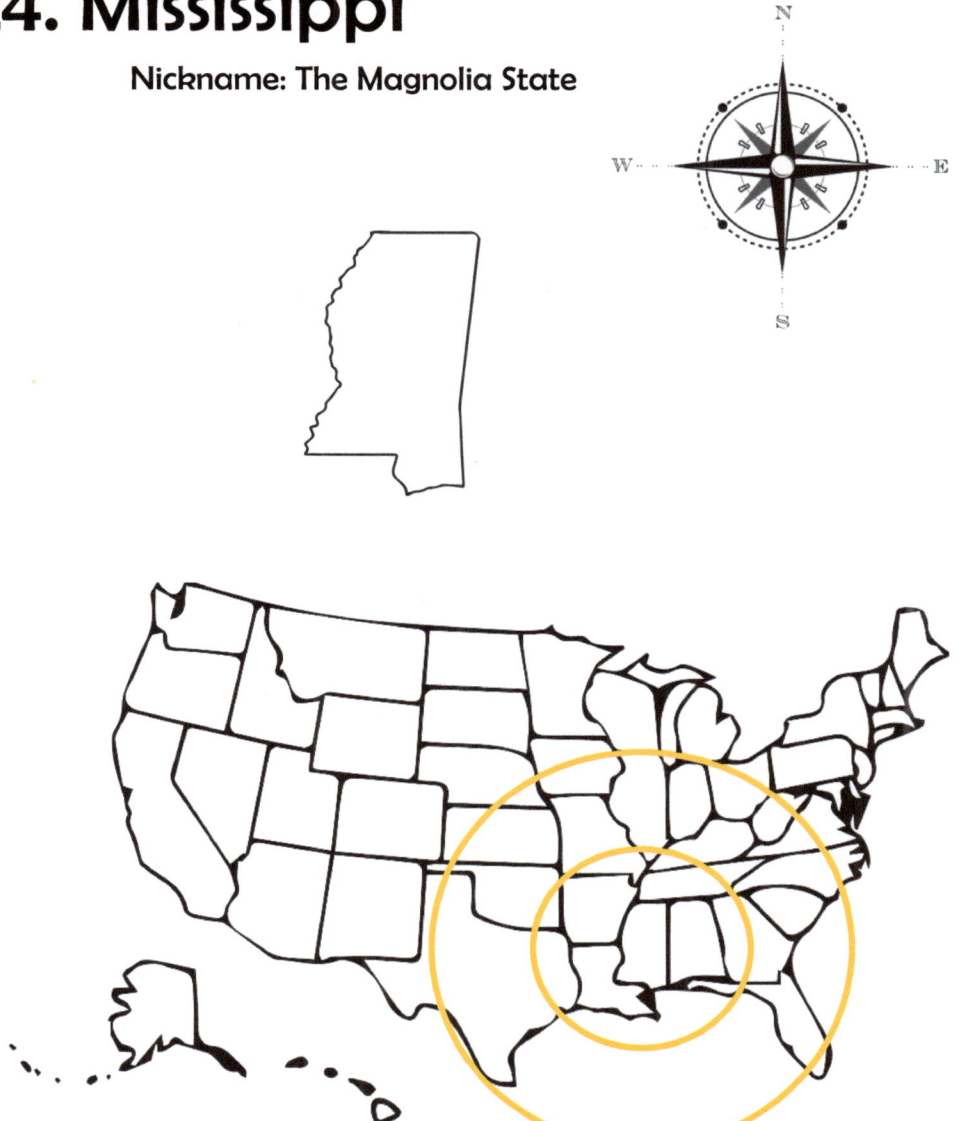

CAPITAL: Jackson

For breakfast try biscuits and gravy, served with bacon and eggs.

25. Missouri

Nickname: The Show Me State

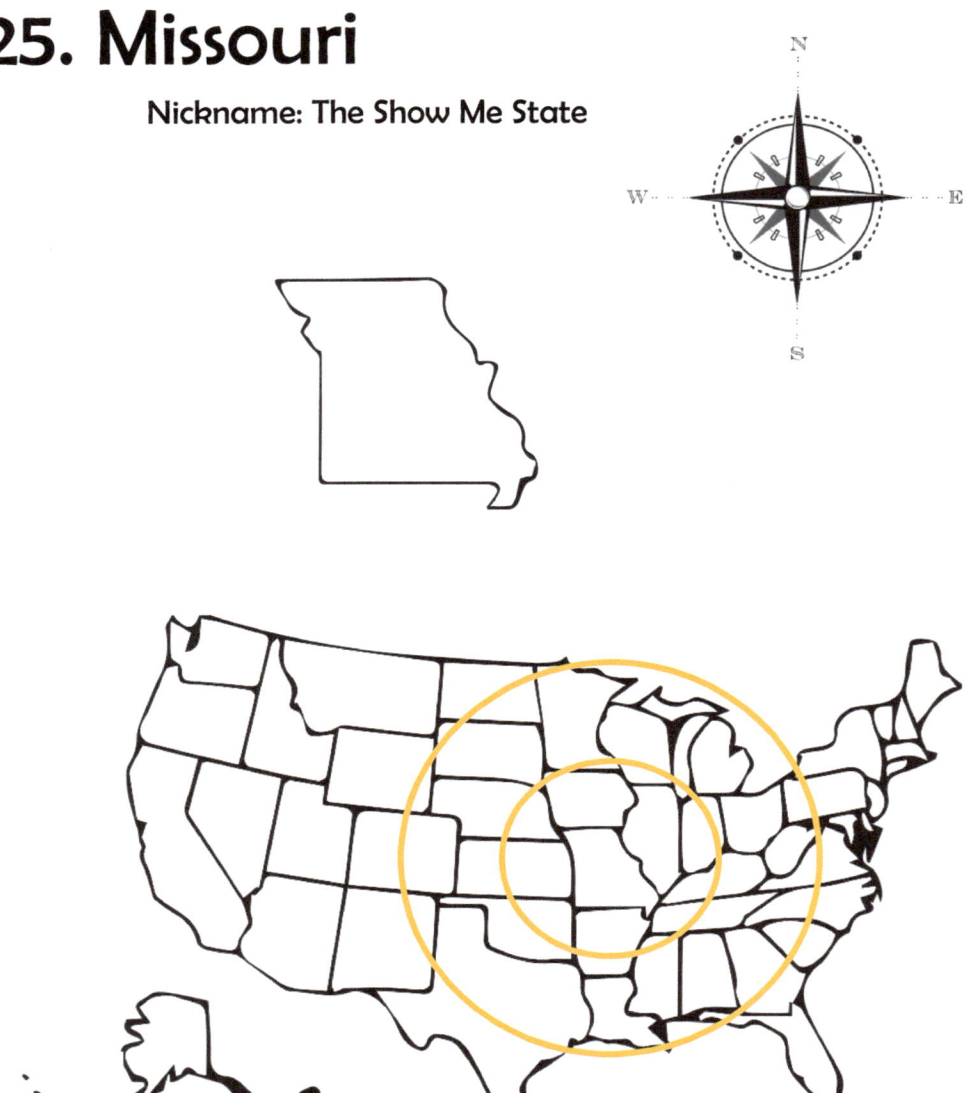

CAPITAL: Jefferson City

Fire up the grill its barbecue time. Missourians love to eat barbecue.

26. Montana

Nickname: The Treasure State

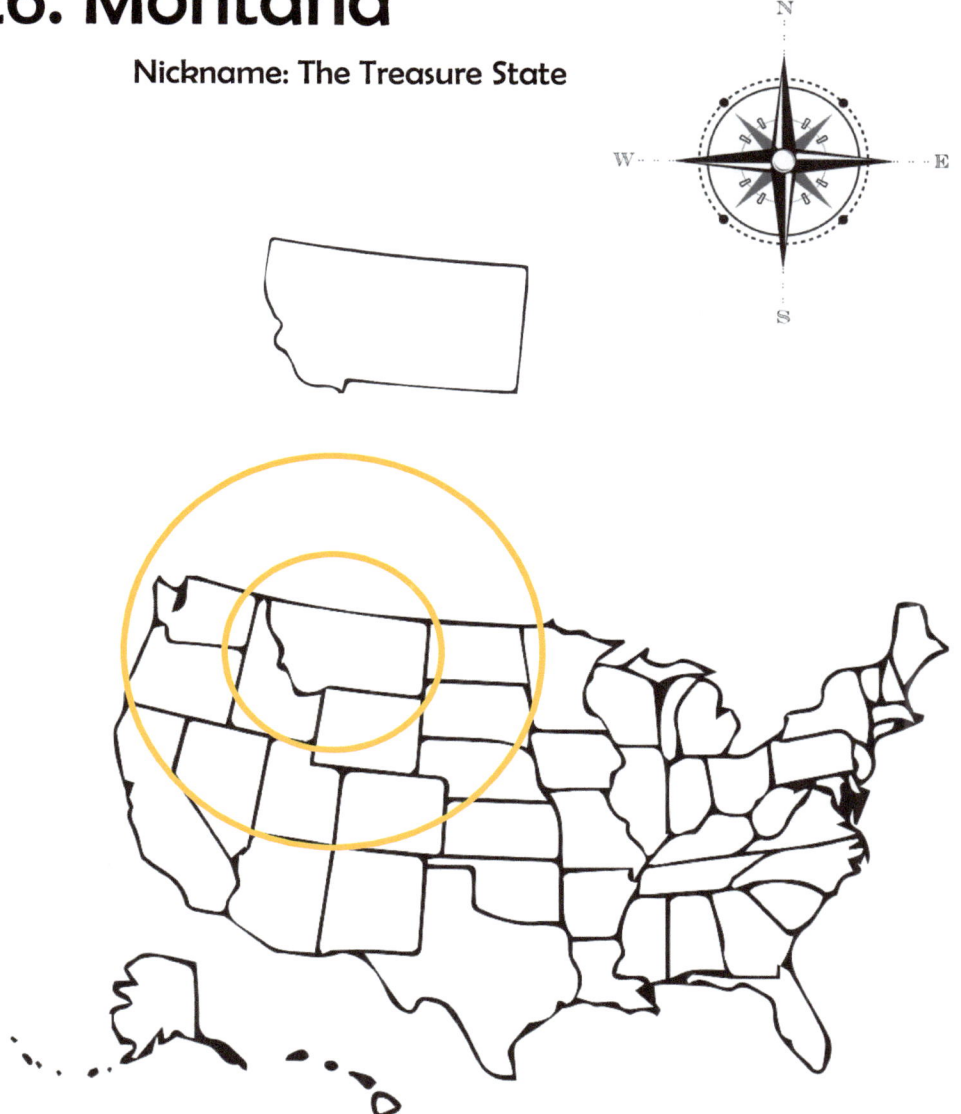

CAPITAL: Helena

A popular appetizer in this state is fried Rocky Mountain oysters.

27. Nebraska

Nickname: The Cornhusker State

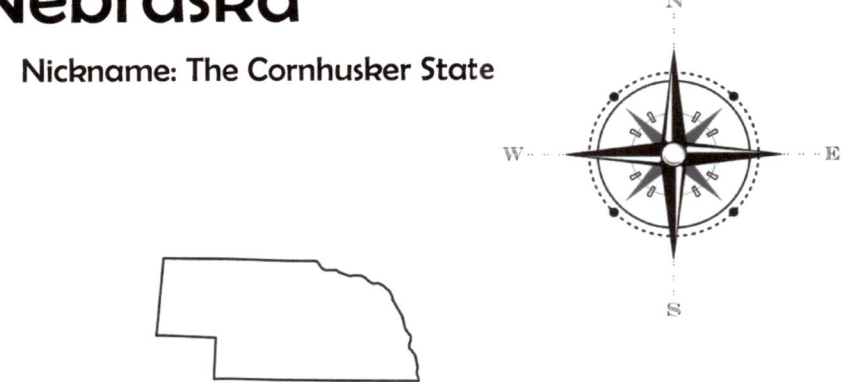

CAPITAL: **Lincoln**

Runza is a traditional dish in Nebraska. A bun stuffed with beef, cabbage, and sautéed onions.

28. Nevada

Nickname: The Silver State

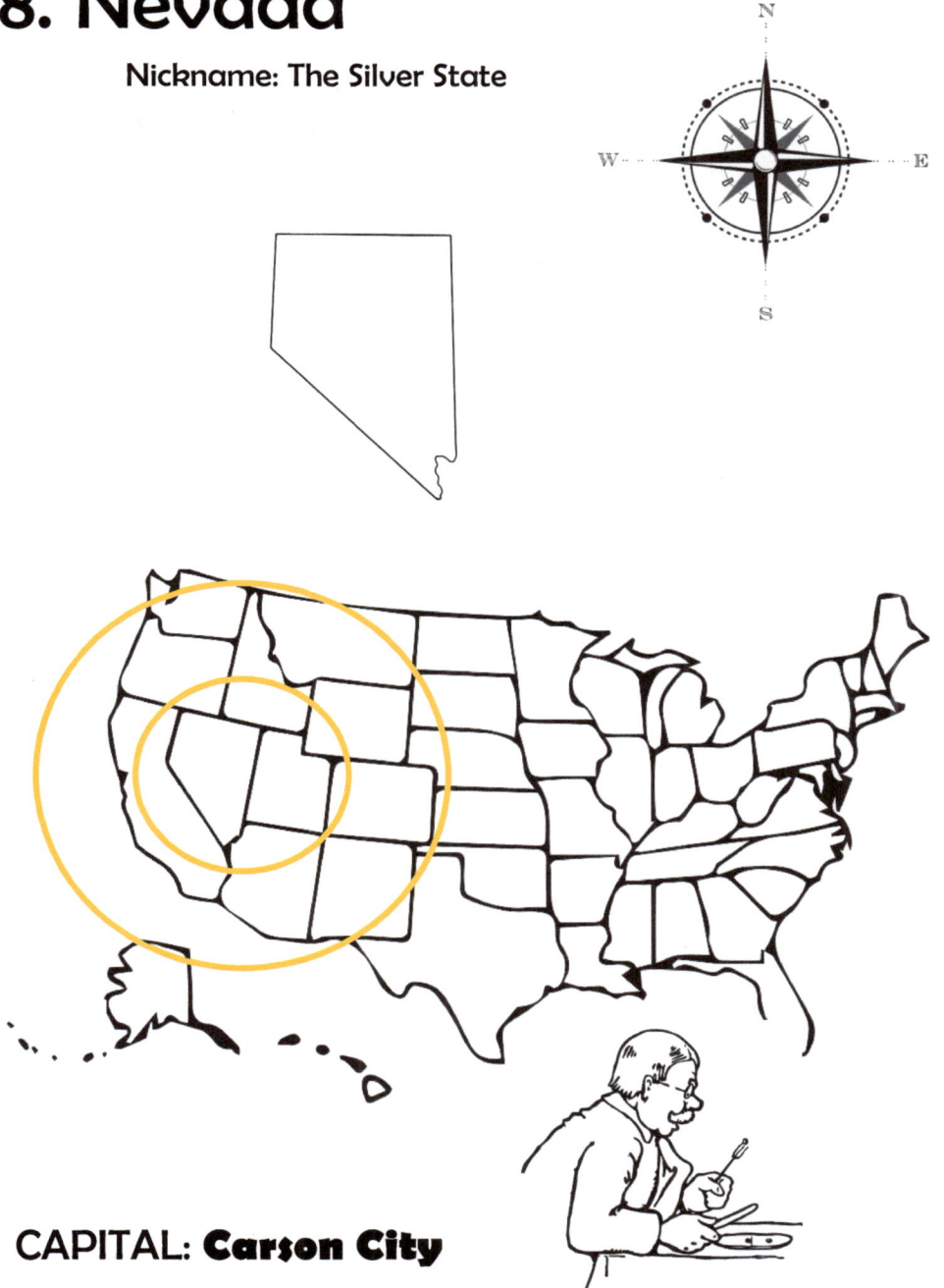

CAPITAL: Carson City

You can satisfy your food cravings at buffet restaurants in Nevada.

29. New Hampshire

Nickname: The Granite State

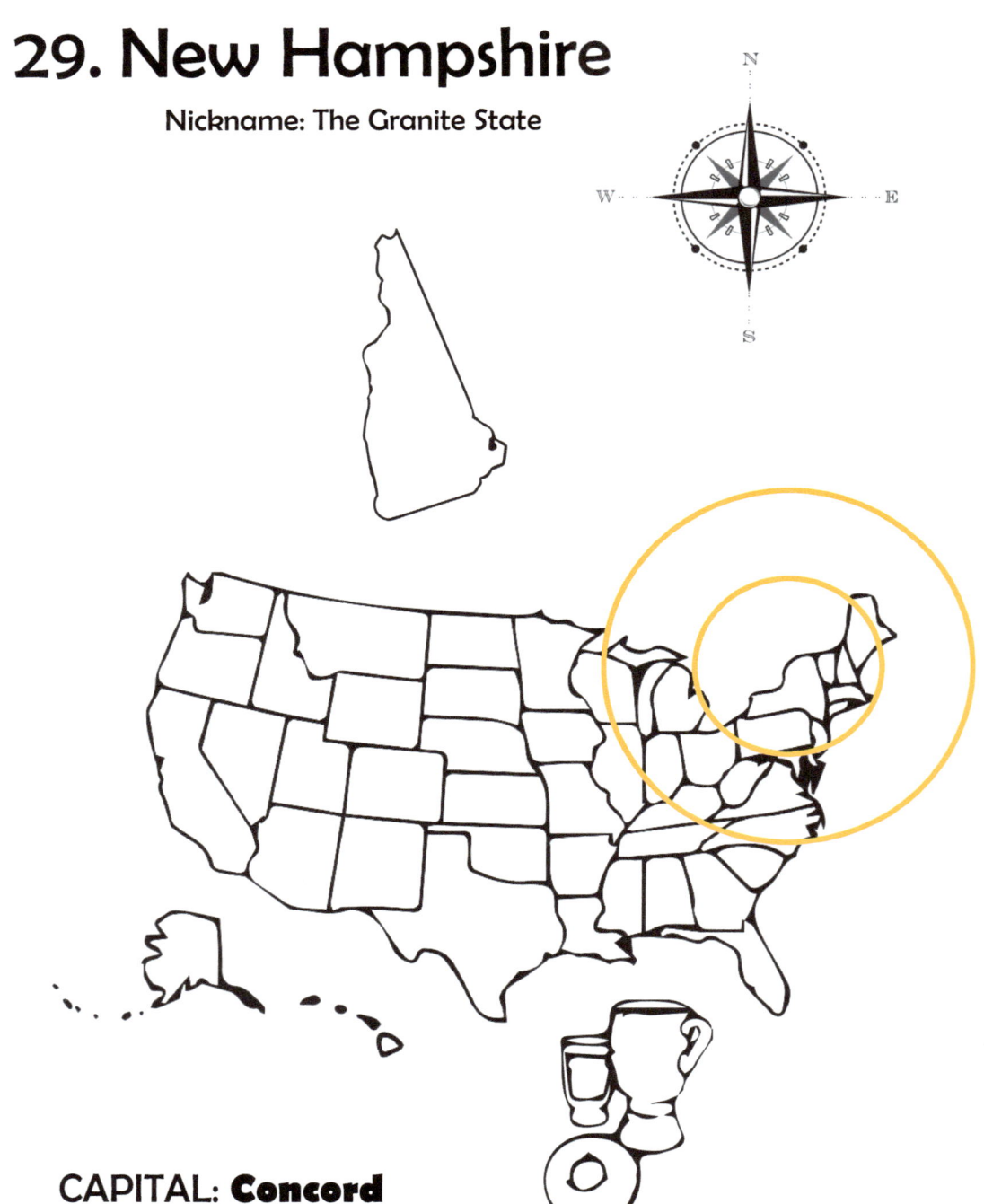

CAPITAL: Concord

When you arrive in New Hampshire have a cider doughnut with tea or coffee.

30. New Jersey

Nickname: The Garden State

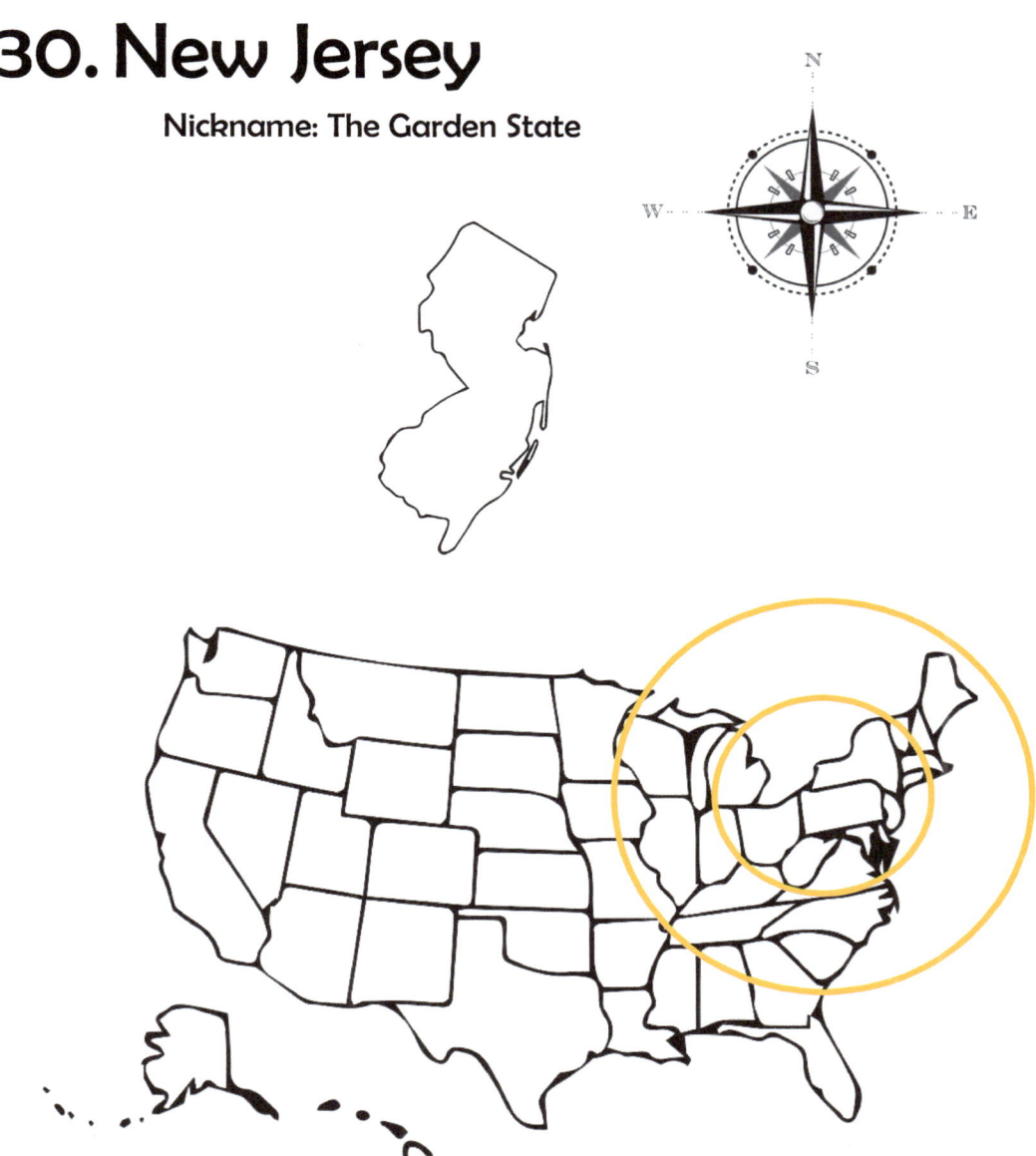

CAPITAL: Trenton

Don't leave New Jersey without buying some saltwater taffy to share with friends and family.

31. New Mexico

Nickname: The Land of Enchantment

CAPITAL: **Santa Fe**

This state is known for its green chile. New Mexicans use green chile to make unique dishes, such as: green chile salsa.

32. New York

Nickname: The Empire State

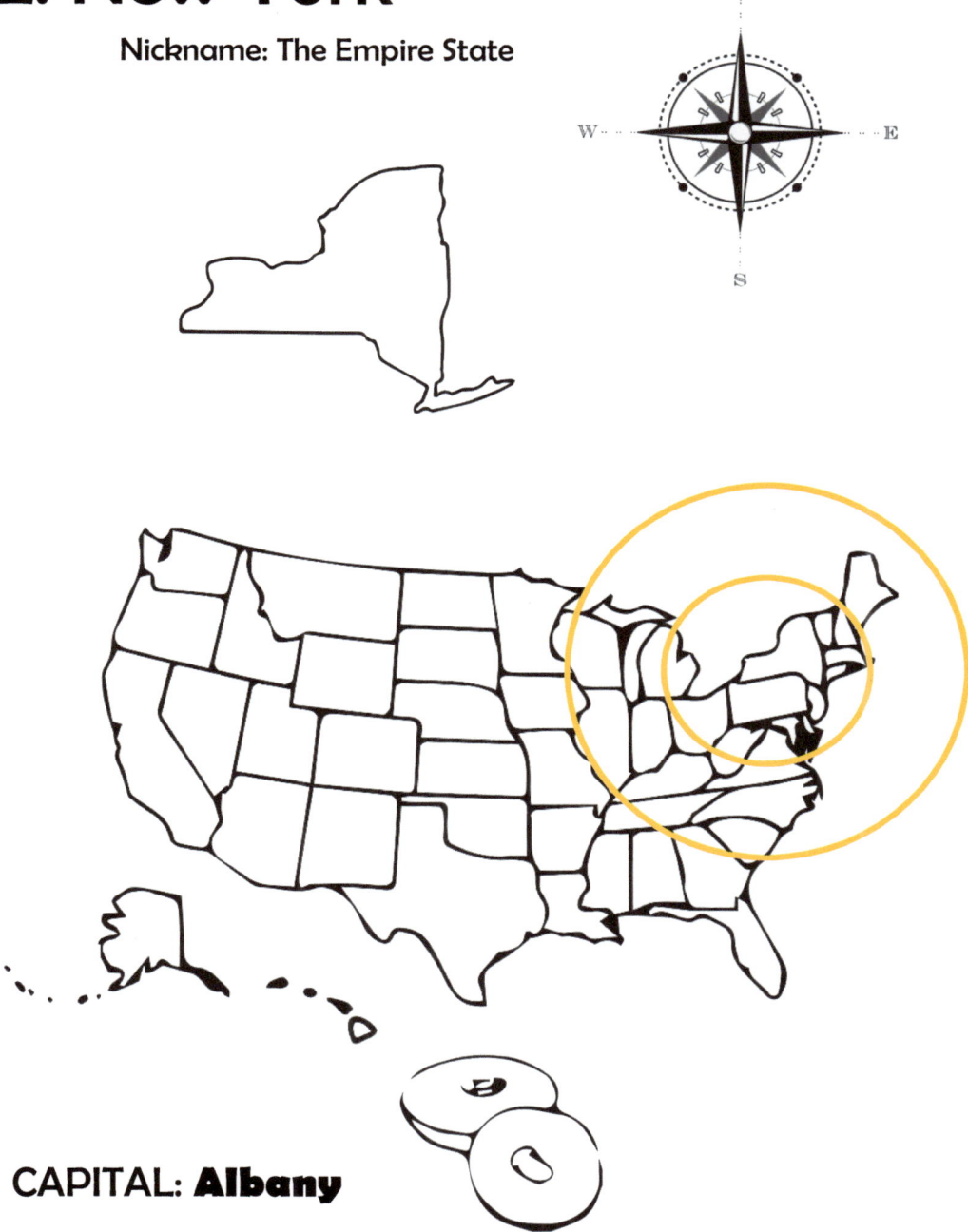

CAPITAL: Albany

Start your day with a fresh, chewy New York bagel.

33. North Carolina

Nickname: The Tar Heel State

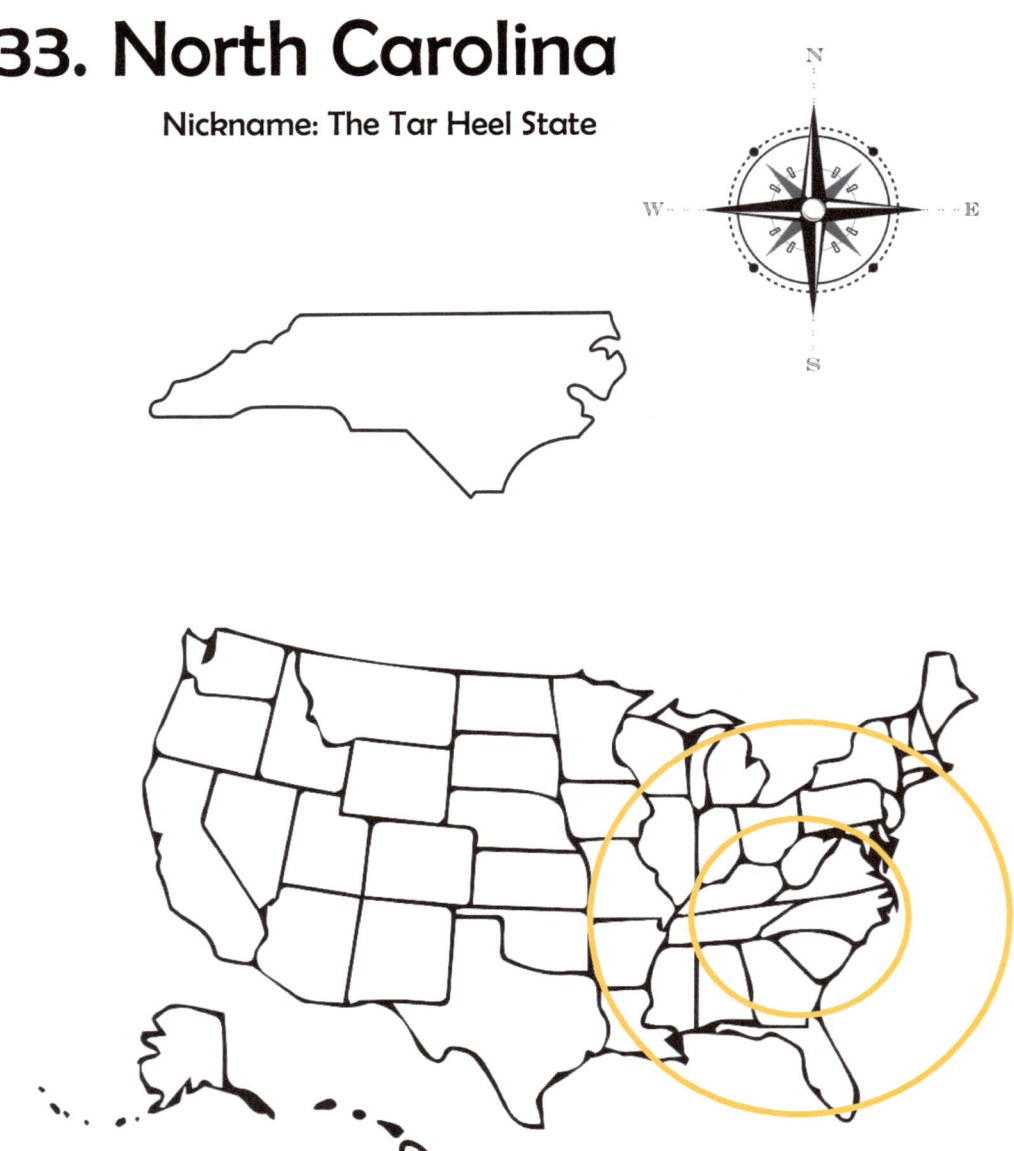

CAPITAL: **Raleigh**

Pork is meat that comes from a pig. Barbecue pork is a classic in this state.

34. North Dakota

Nickname: The Peace Garden State

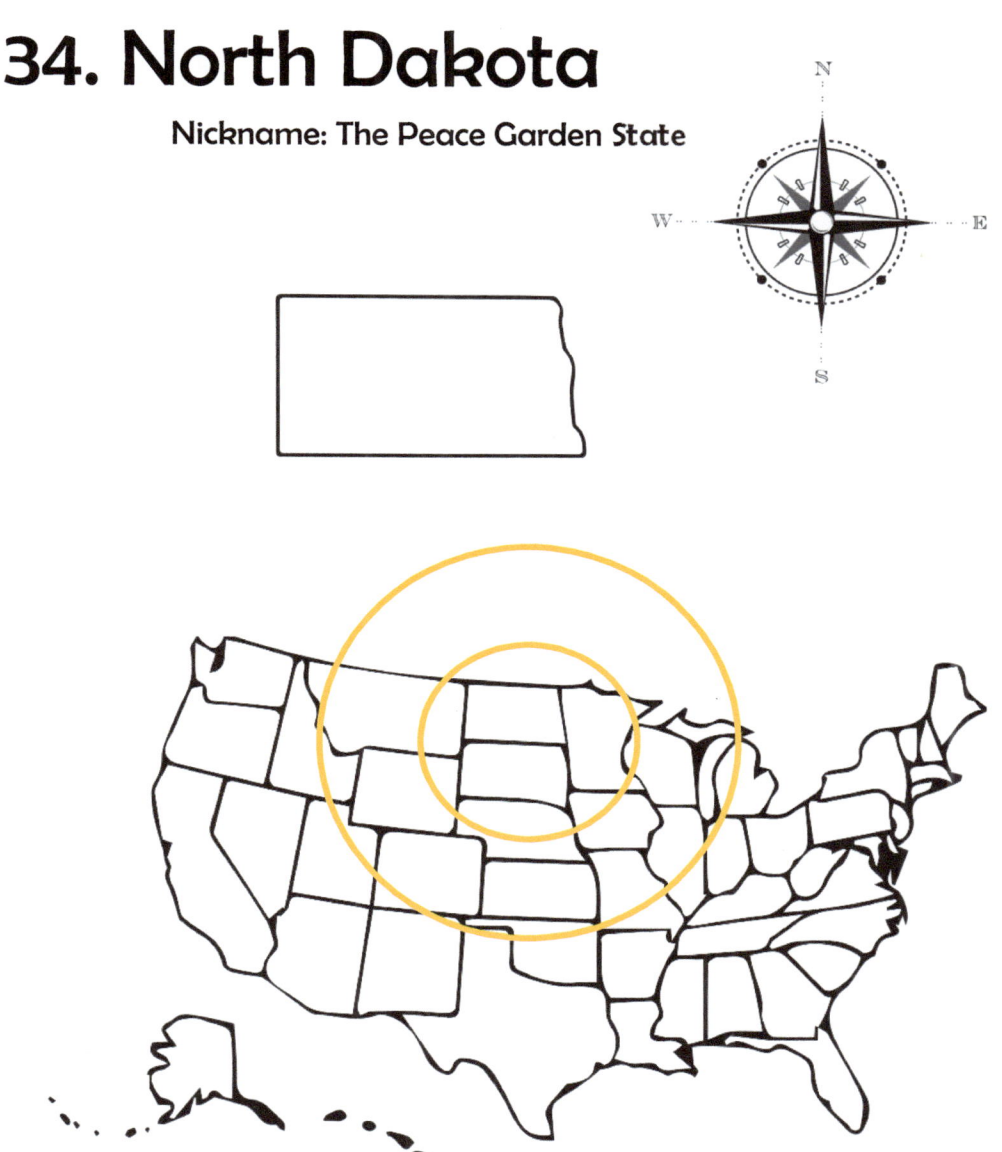

CAPITAL: Bismarck

Try Bison burgers when you arrive in this state.

35. Ohio

Nickname: The Buckeye State

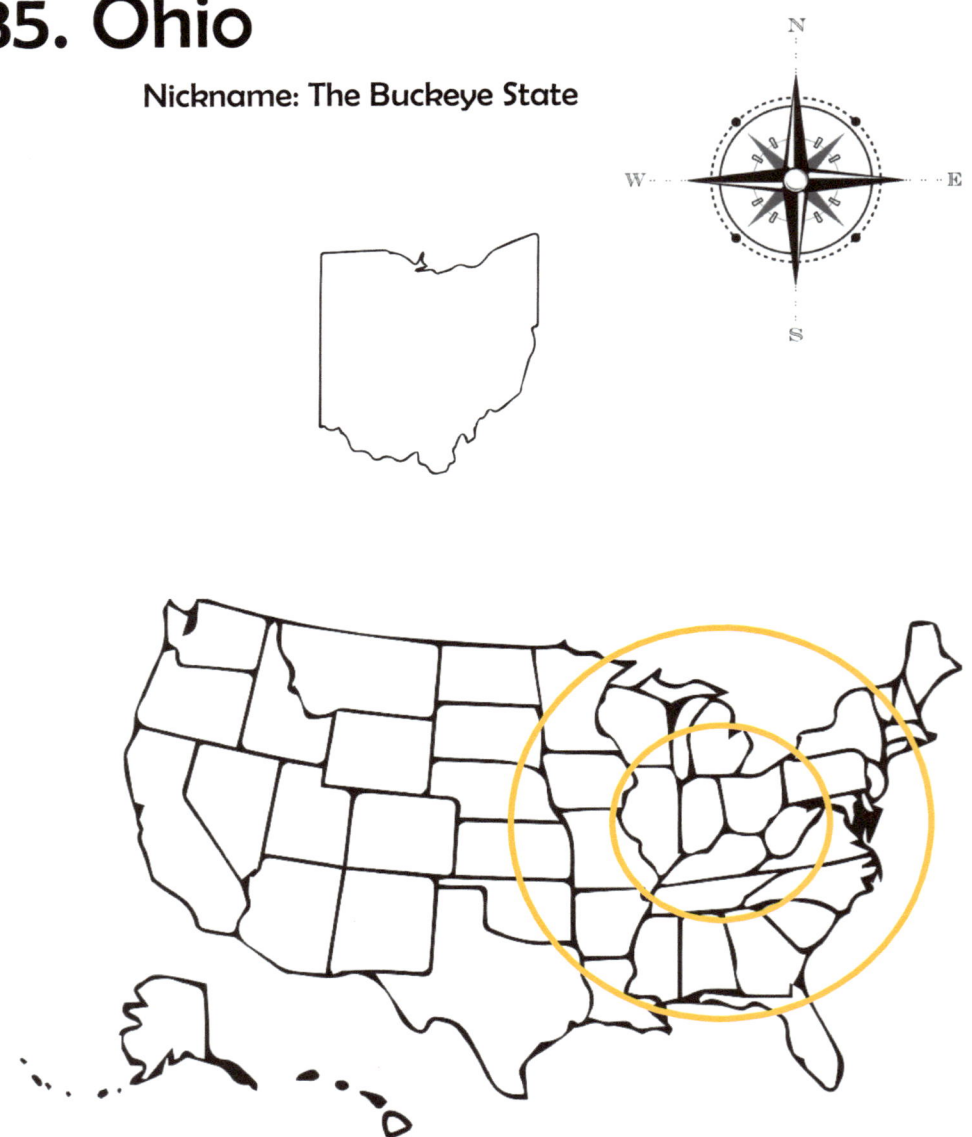

CAPITAL: **Columbus**

Ohioans love buckeyes with peanut butter and chocolate.

36. Oklahoma

Nickname: The Sooner State

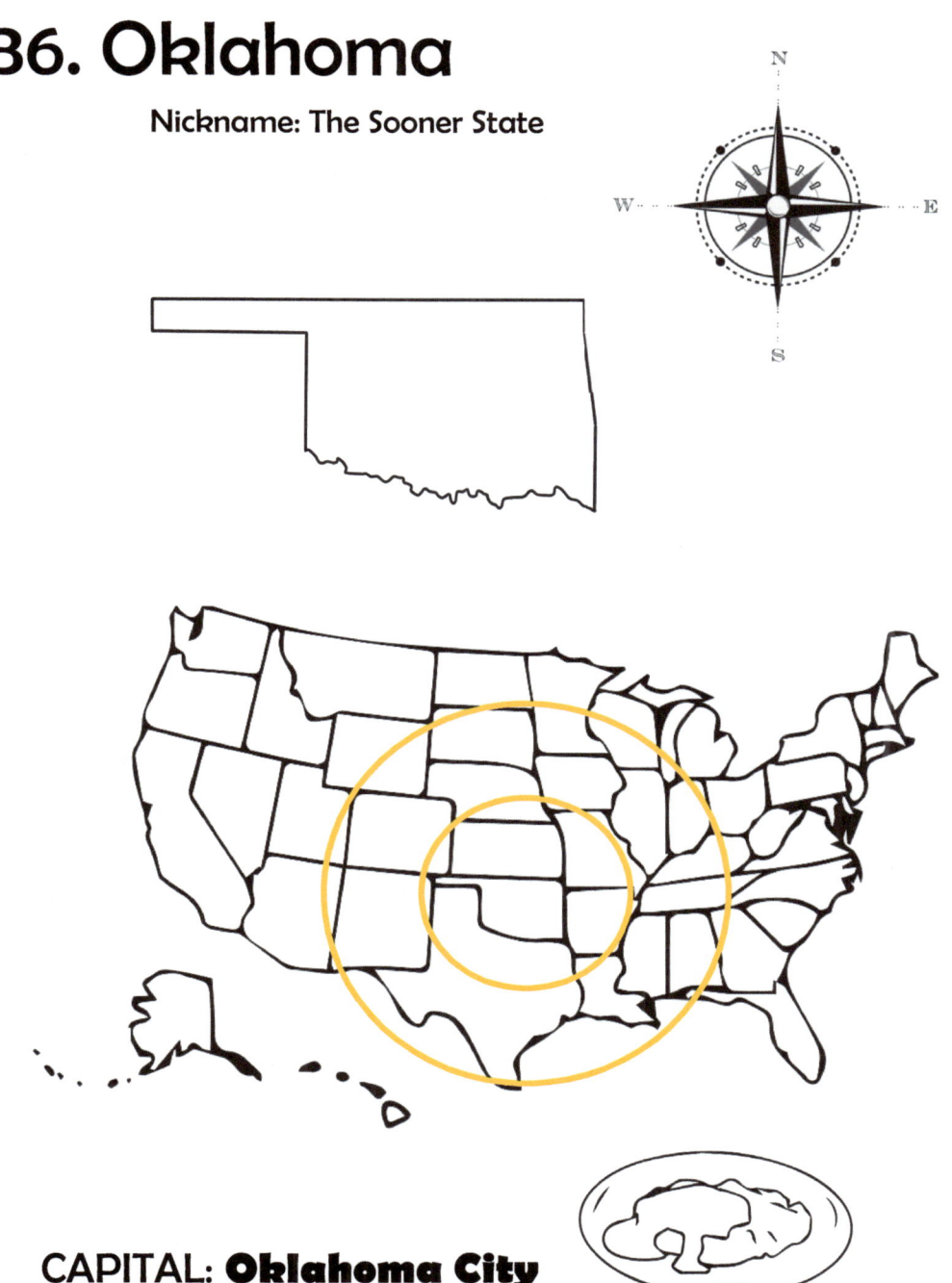

CAPITAL: Oklahoma City

Chicken fried steak is a favorite dish in Oklahoma.

37. Oregon

Nickname: The Beaver State

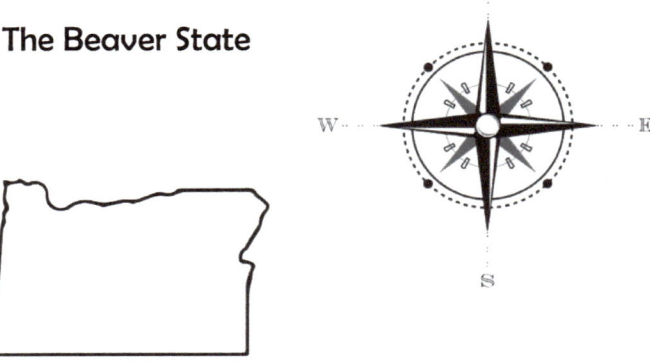

CAPITAL: **Salem**

Marionberries are serving for dessert.

38. Pennsylvania

Nickname: The Keystone State

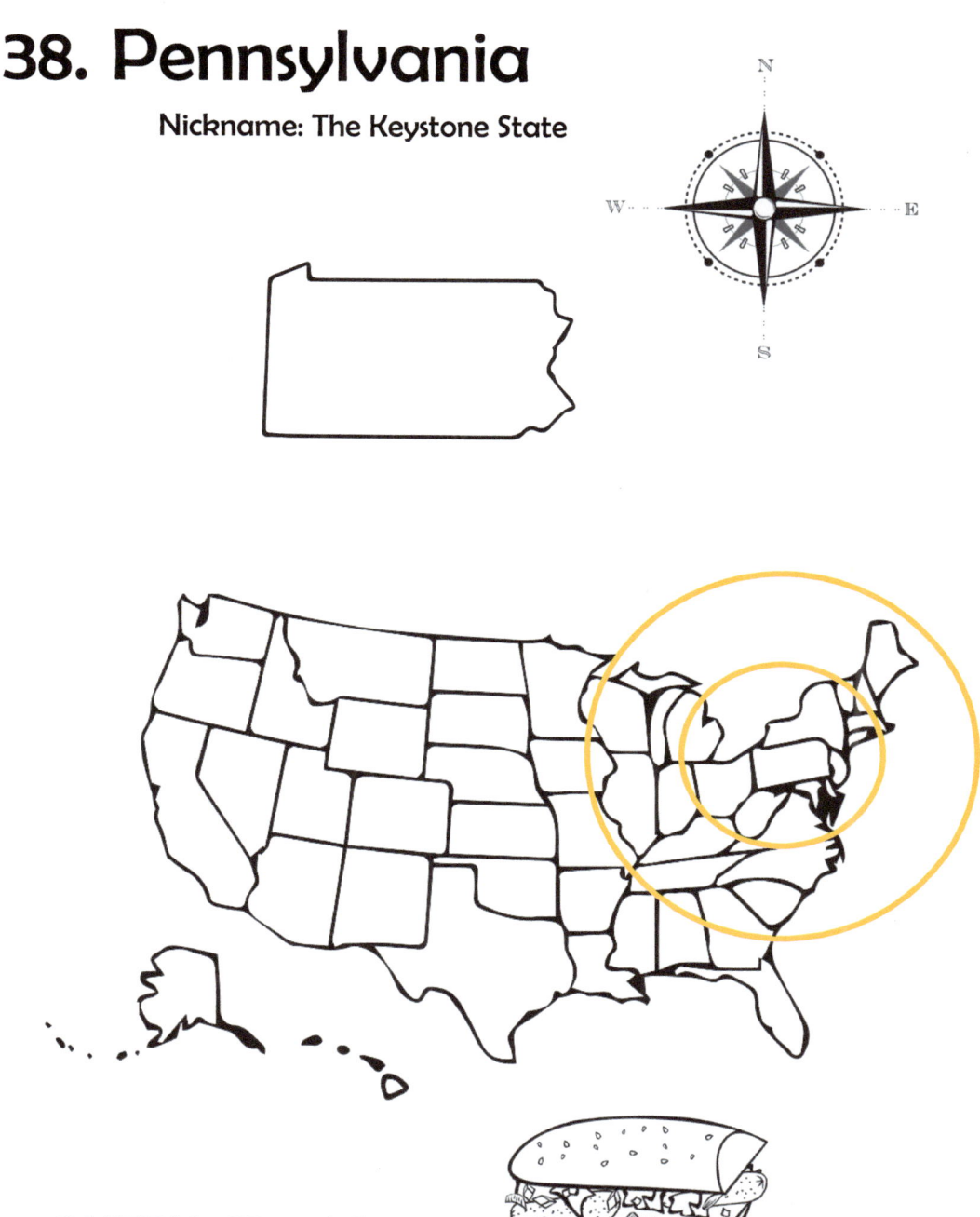

CAPITAL: Harrisburg

For lunch, try a toasted Philly cheesesteak.

39. Rhode Island

Nickname: The Ocean State

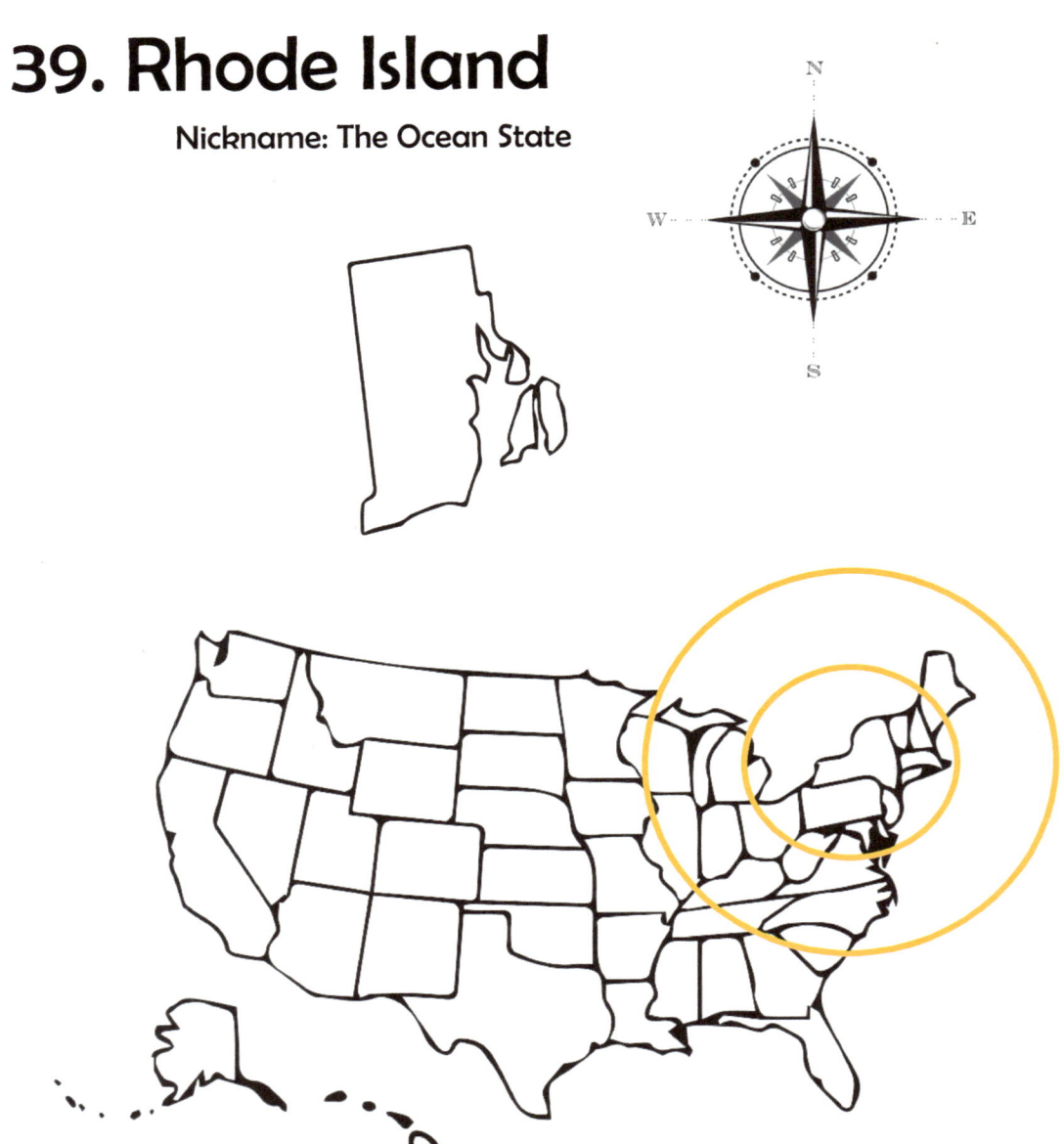

CAPITAL: **Providence**

In the summer, clam cakes or clam fritters are plentiful.

40. South Carolina

Nickname: The Palmetto State

CAPITAL: Columbia

Satisfy your thirst, on a hot day, with South Carolina sweet tea.

41. South Dakota

Nickname: Mount Rushmore State

CAPITAL: Pierre

Grandma makes the best Kuchen pie, filled with fruit and custard.

42. Tennessee

Nickname: The Volunteer State

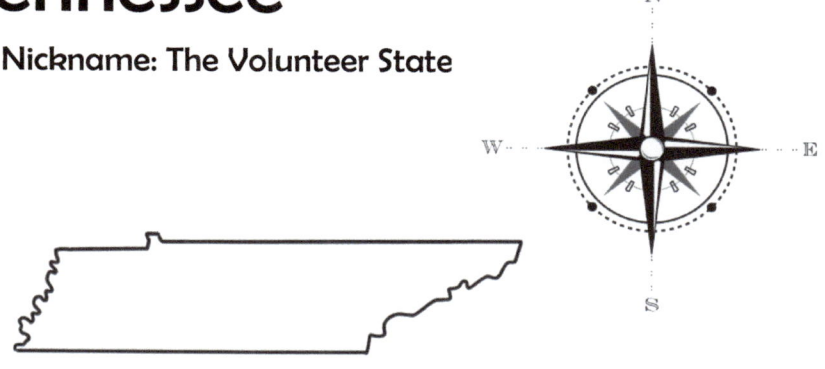

CAPITAL: Nashville

Cayenne-based pepper chicken, known as "Hot Chicken," is a popular dish in Tennessee.

43. Texas

Nickname: The Lone Star State

CAPITAL: Austin

Tex Mex is a cheesy Mexican dish Texans love.

44. Utah

Nickname: The Beehive State

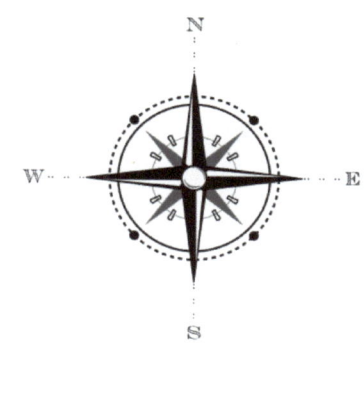

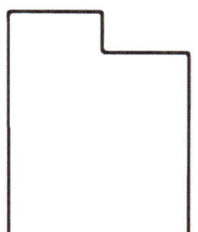

CAPITAL: Salt Lake City

Utah is famous for Jell-O in many different flavors.

45. Vermont

Nickname: The Green Mountain State

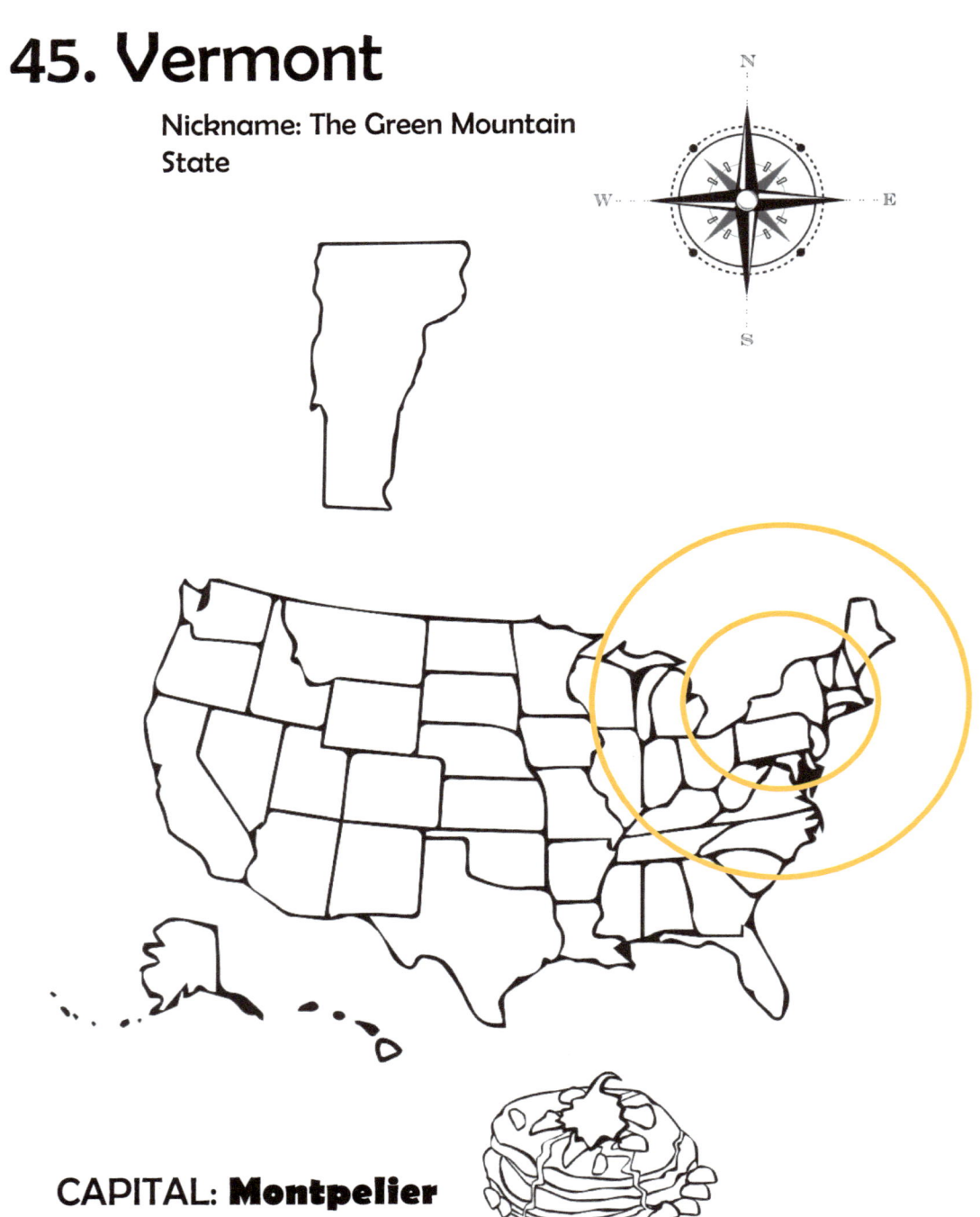

CAPITAL: Montpelier

You can top your pancakes with maple syrup from Vermont.

46. Virginia

Nickname: The Old Dominion State

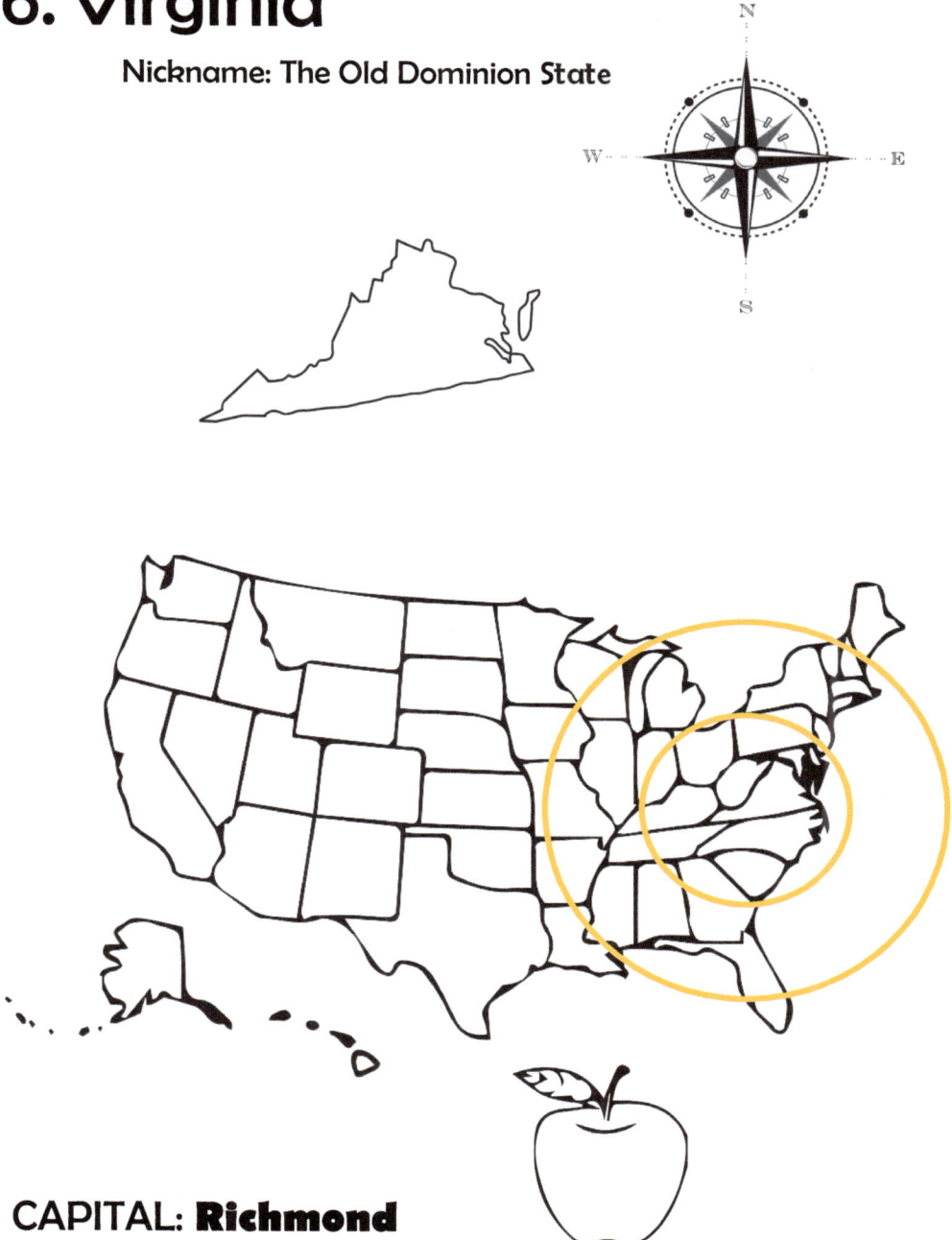

CAPITAL: Richmond

An apple a day keeps the doctor away. Pick apples from the orchards in Virginia or grow them in your backyard.

47. Washington

Nickname: The Evergreen State

CAPITAL: **Olympia**

On a cold winter morning, a bowl of pho will help warm you up. This Vietnamese noodle soup is a tradition in Washington.

48. West Virginia

Nickname: The Mountain State

CAPITAL: Charleston

Try a West Virginia pepperoni roll. A popular meal for miners in that state.

49. Wisconsin

Nickname: The Badger State

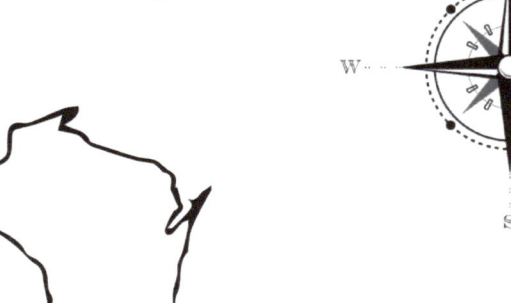

CAPITAL: Madison

Cheese is a Wisconsin tradition. So many cheeses to choose from in this state.

50. Wyoming

Nickname: The Equality or Cowboy State

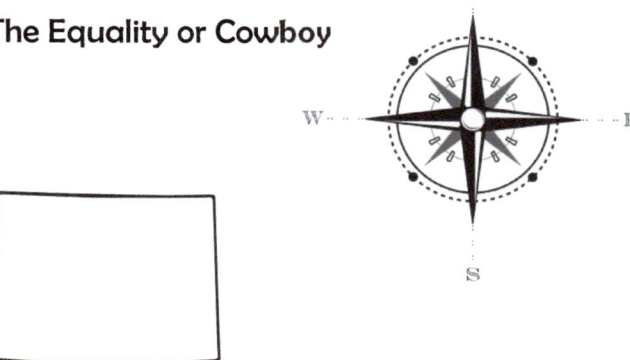

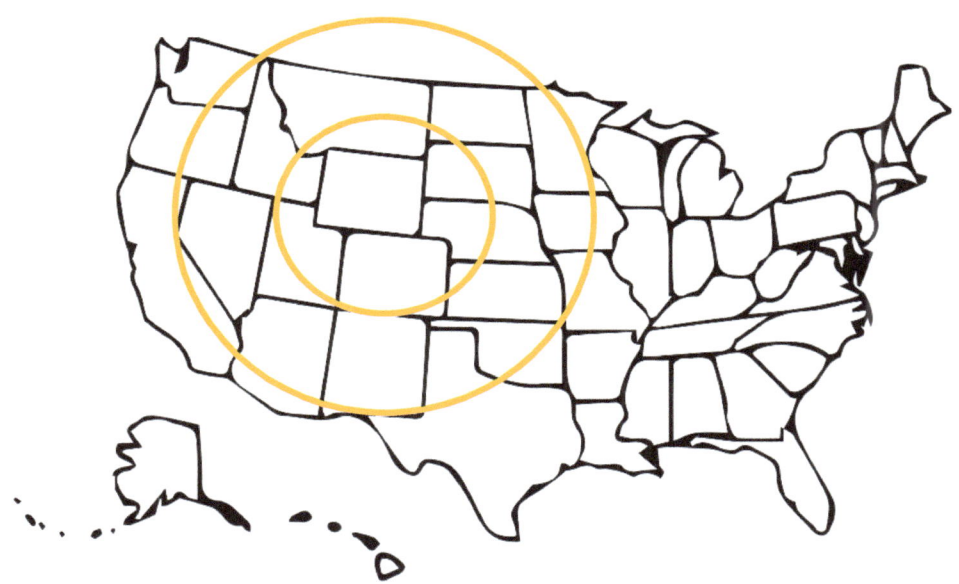

CAPITAL: **Cheyenne**

In Wyoming, Beef Jerky is a popular snack. It comes in many flavors, such as smoked, peppered, and honey.

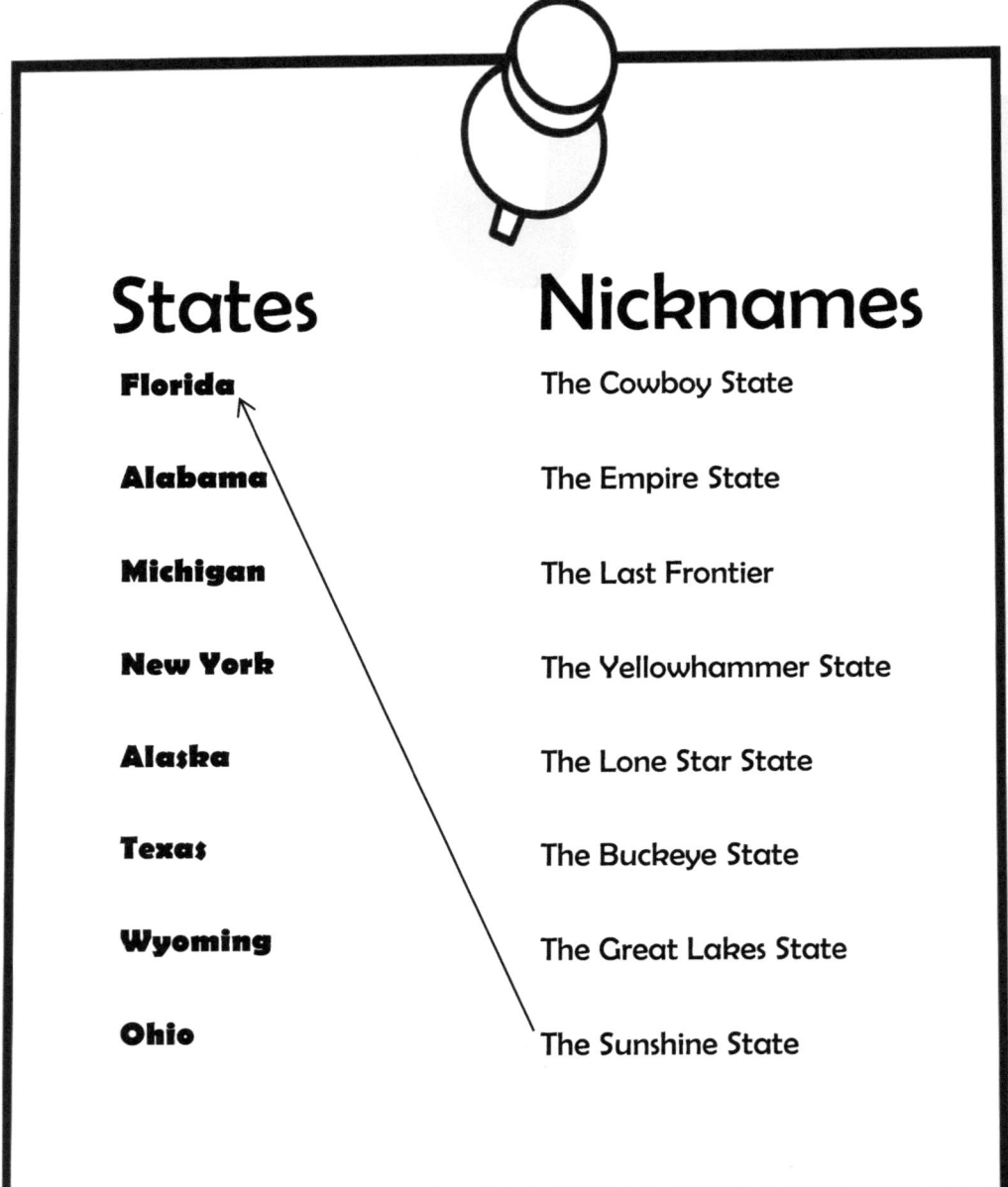

States	Nicknames
Florida	The Cowboy State
Alabama	The Empire State
Michigan	The Last Frontier
New York	The Yellowhammer State
Alaska	The Lone Star State
Texas	The Buckeye State
Wyoming	The Great Lakes State
Ohio	The Sunshine State

Matching Exercise

Match the nickname with the appropriate state. Draw a line to make the connections.

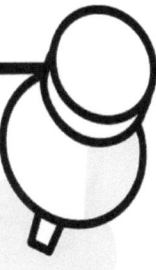

States

Arizona

New Jersey

Arkansas

California

Georgia

Colorado

Kansas

Maryland

Nicknames

The Centennial State

The Peach State

The Grand Canyon State

The Sunflower State

The Garden State

The Old Line State

The Natural State

The Golden State

Matching Exercise

Match the nickname with the appropriate state. Draw a line to make the connections.

States · Nicknames

States	Nicknames
Connecticut	The Sooner State
Idaho	The Pelican State
Hawaii	The Gem State
Delaware	The Constitution State
Wisconsin	The Hawkeye State
Louisiana	The First State
Iowa	The Badger State
Oklahoma	The Aloha State

Matching Exercise

Match the nickname with the appropriate state. Draw a line to make the connections.

States	Nicknames
Illinois	The Magnolia State
Massachusetts	The Palmetto State
North Dakota	The Bay State
Mississippi	The Prairie State
North Carolina	The Ocean State
South Dakota	Mount Rushmore State
South Carolina	The Peace Garden State
Rhode Island	The Tar Heel State

Matching Exercise

Match the nickname with the appropriate state. Draw a line to make the connections.

States	Nicknames
Nevada	The Land of Enchantment
Missouri	The Evergreen State
Nebraska	The Cornhusker State
Tennessee	The Mountain State
Washington	The Volunteer State
Vermont	The Green Mountain State
West Virginia	The Silver State
New Mexico	The Show Me State

Matching Exercise

Match the nickname with the appropriate state. Draw a line to make the connections.

States	Nicknames
Indiana	The Pine Tree State
Kentucky	The Treasure State
Maine	The North Star State
Minnesota	The Hoosier State
Montana	The Granite State
Oregon	The Bluegrass State
New Hampshire	The Keystone State
Pennsylvania	The Beaver State

Matching Exercise

Match the nickname with the appropriate state. Draw a line to make the connections.

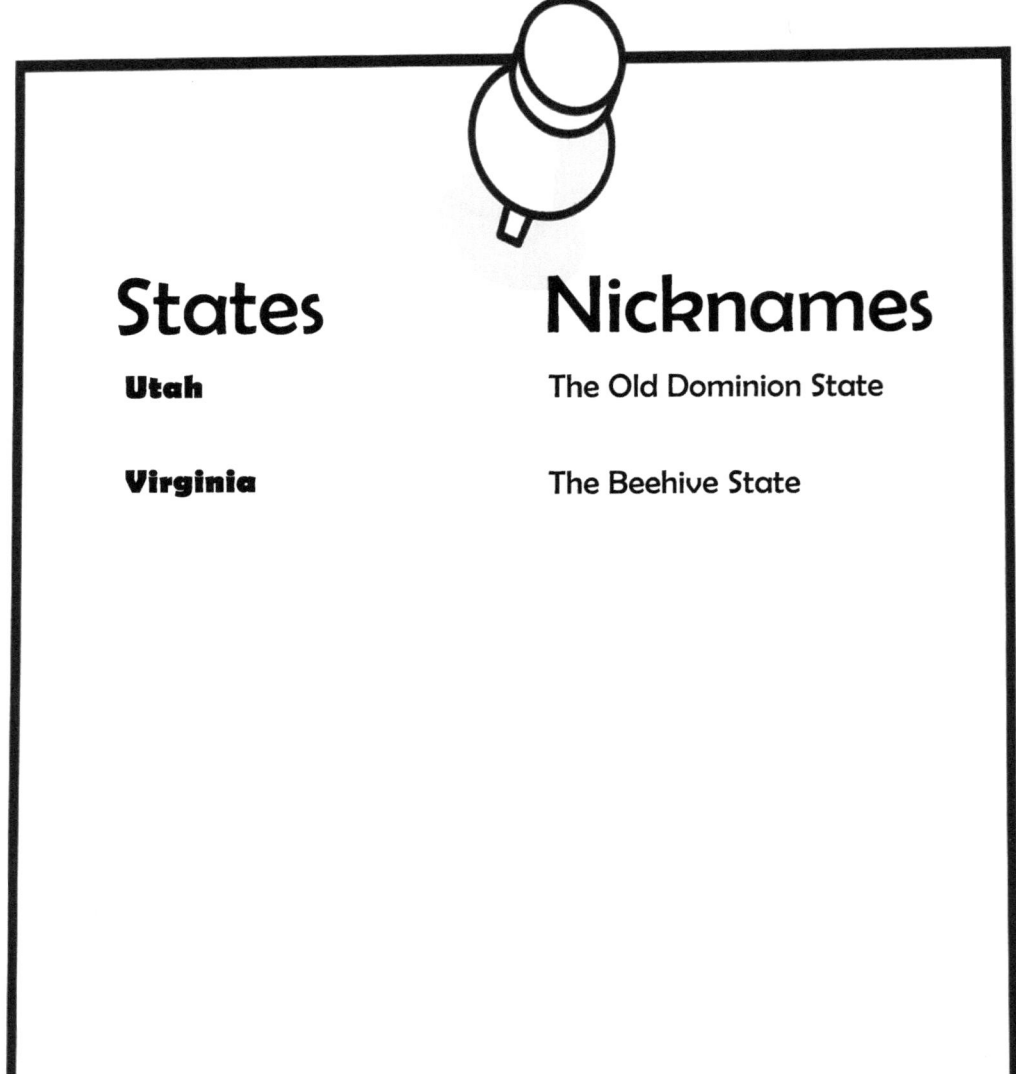

Matching Exercise

Match the nickname with the appropriate state. Draw a line to make the connections.

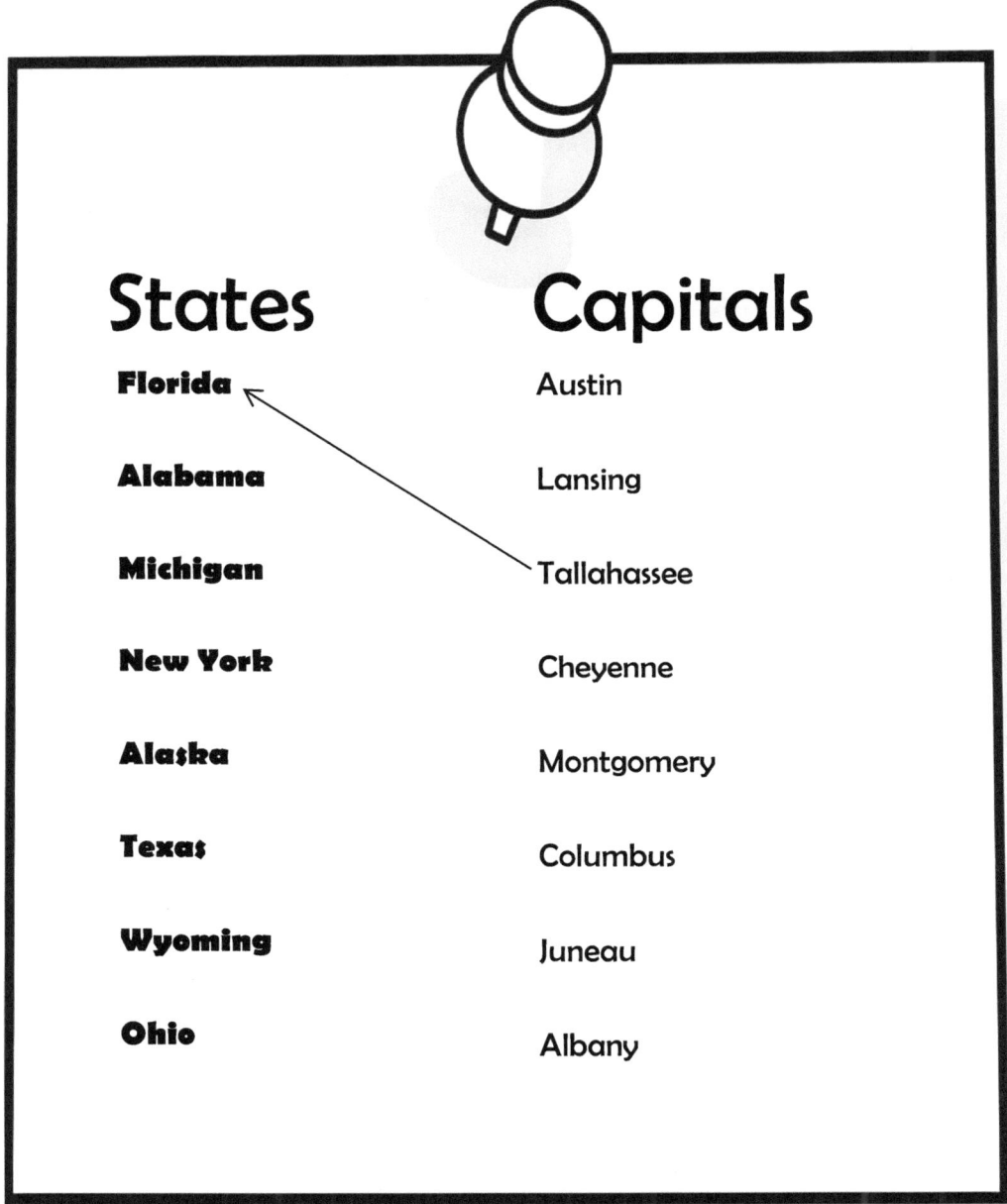

States	Capitals
Florida	Austin
Alabama	Lansing
Michigan	Tallahassee
New York	Cheyenne
Alaska	Montgomery
Texas	Columbus
Wyoming	Juneau
Ohio	Albany

Matching Exercise

Match the capital with the appropriate state. Draw a line to make the connections.

States   Capitals

Arizona   Little Rock

New Jersey   Trenton

Arkansas   Topeka

California   Phoenix

Georgia   Denver

Colorado   Sacramento

Kansas   Annapolis

Maryland   Atlanta

Matching Exercise

Match the capital with the appropriate state. Draw a line to make the connections.

States	Capitals
Connecticut	Des Moines
Idaho	Dover
Hawaii	Madison
Delaware	Boise
Wisconsin	Hartford
Louisiana	Honolulu
Iowa	Oklahoma City
Oklahoma	Baton Rouge

Matching Exercise

Match the capital with the appropriate state. Draw a line to make the connections.

States   Capitals

Illinois   Bismarck

Massachusetts   Pierre

North Dakota   Springfield

Mississippi   Jackson

North Carolina   Columbia

South Dakota   Mount

South Carolina   Providence

Rhode Island   Raleigh

Matching Exercise

Match the capital with the appropriate state. Draw a line to make the connections.

States

Nevada

Missouri

Nebraska

Tennessee

Washington

Vermont

West Virginia

New Mexico

Capitals

Olympia

Jefferson City

Montpelier

Carson City

Santa Fe

Nashville

Lincoln

Charleston

Matching Exercise

Match the capital with the appropriate state. Draw a line to make the connections.

States   Capitals

States	Capitals
Indiana	Harrisburg
Kentucky	Augusta
Maine	Salem
Minnesota	Indianapolis
Montana	Concord
Oregon	Helena
New Hampshire	Frankfort
Pennsylvania	St. Paul

Matching Exercise

Match the capital with the appropriate state. Draw a line to make the connections.

States

Utah

Virginia

Capitals

Richmond

Salt Lake City

Matching Exercise

Match the capitals with the appropriate state. Draw a line to make the connections.

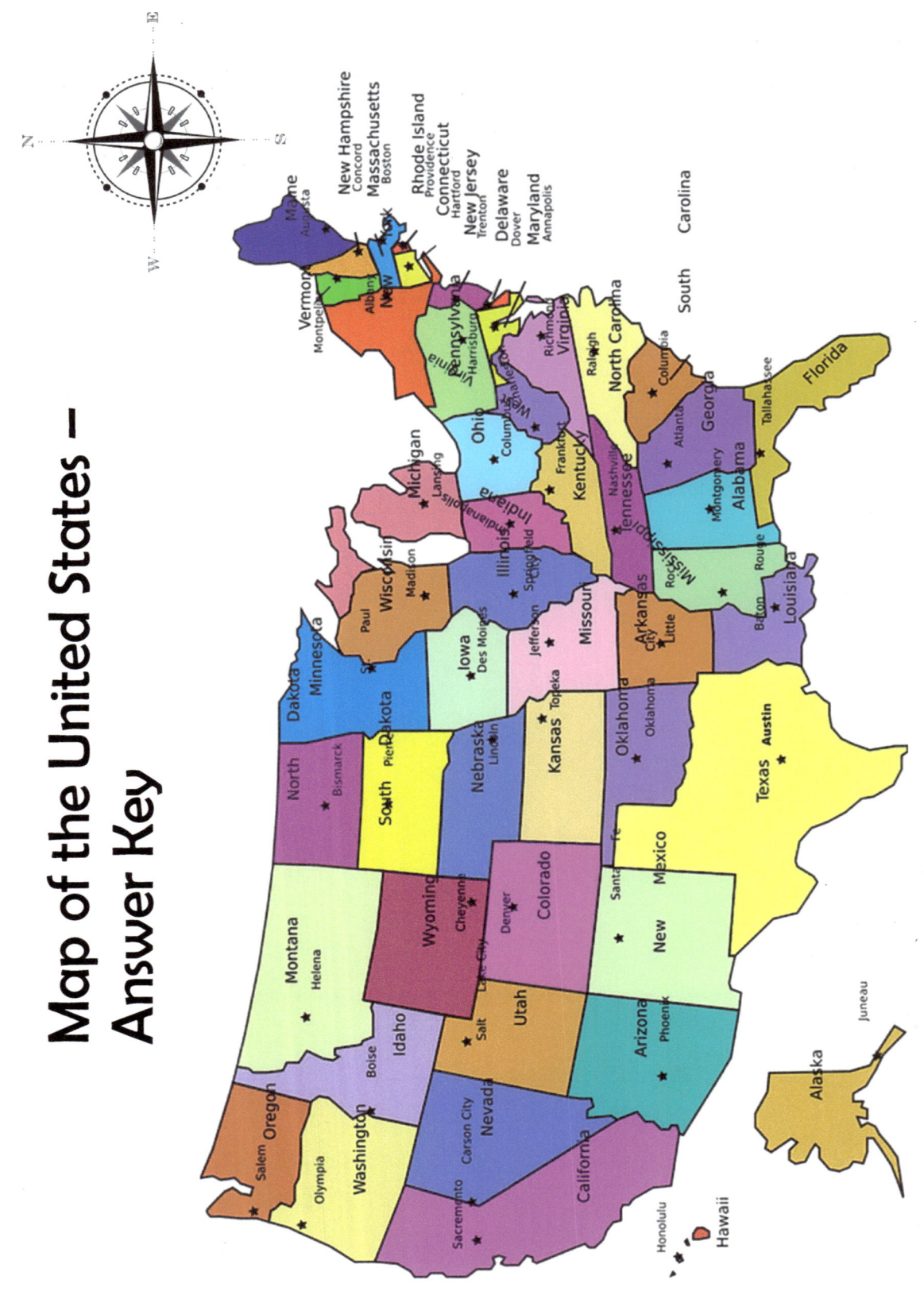